IND.

INTRODUCTION

Do not give up on your dreams is a motivational menthol for those who dream, who have a goal, an objective, but they are afraid, seized by fear, and indecision. It is for those who do not dare run to go in search of that dream which they have had anchored in their minds, and for whatever circumstances have not been able to fight for it, or to make it come true.

Do not give up on your dreams, is for you who has an idea hanging around in your head, and this idea does not have a body or a name yet, the time has come to turn on that little dim light that shines with its own light, it's time to spark it up and not let it burn off.

My intention is that you arm yourself with courage, enthusiasm, leaving behind all the barriers, and the fears.

Put on a warrior's armor to fight your battles. Break the limits of your mind, place yourself on the path of opportunity, alongside of efforts, work, dedication, commitment, and good preparation, change your reality with the power of your thinking, a positive and tenacious mind is capable of overcoming barriers, obstacles and removing the biggest debris from the road.

Do not give up on your dreams is a spark of courage, an urge to dream, to believe, to persevere, to work, to study, and not stop, its dress for success.

Do not give up your dreams

MODESTA MATA

Do not give up on your dreams

Many times life is a little complicated for some people, so much so that those who have dreams give up on them because they do not see the light of hope that points out a small way, to be able to go ahead with that vision or idea they have; in the face of so many failures, defeats and difficulties, many have wondered why this terrible situation is happening to them, but the truth is that the majority of those who we can see today around the world be prosperous, happy and triumphant, have had to face horrible moments, where in one way or another it has marked their lives and that of their families, only thing is, they have not allowed themselves to be frightened by the adversities that have been presented to them in their journey through life, to you dear reader I invite you to dream, to raise your head, to look up with enthusiasm and determination.

It does not matter what your dreams are, put them into practice, pursue your dreams, work hard, but you cannot run then walk, do not stop, avoid falling into discouragement, it is the only enemy that could stop success, believe that, it is possible, even if things in your life are not coming out as expected; fainting, prevents further fighting, get up, regain strength. It is possible that the mountain top you dream of reaching is far away, or too high, but no matter how far away it may seem, and even if you do not have the skill for climbing mountains, you can reach the top of the summit, just do not look at how sublime or elevated it is.

The climber when he decides to climb a mountain, he never measures its height, he only goes in search of his dream: to climb; and when he happens to slip, falling down, he simply gets back on his feet. He sets off again, continues ascending with hard work, no matter how obviously dangerous and exhausting, and intricate his journey to the top will be, just to see his dream come true. You, along with all of us can imitate the alpinist, he never gives up on his dreams, he continues on despite the roughness, and inaccessible upland. He does not allow himself to be crushed and much less crushed by the stones that come off trying to keep him from going up. I invite you to take a nice walk in the beautiful garden of dreams, dare to dream, dreams can come true, begin with yours, persist, give a thought, set a little idea in your head.

Never stop trying, do not give yourself into believing that your dream is too small, perhaps you have observed the farmers with a small grain of corn that they plant into the dirt and get thousands and millions of grains more, gather up the courage, the effort, the determination, the perseverance and patience to wait for the dream, after its hard work begins to bear fruit, but needs the necessary tools, a dose of optimism, enthusiasm, motivation, together with continuous and meticulous work, it all plays a very important role when you want to achieve something.

We must not forget that for a dream to become a reality, certain rules apply, as in almost everything in our journey within this small ship called the world. If someone wants to be a good citizen must maintain a good behavior in accordance with the rules established in his community, he who thinks to be a doctor must first study, everything that is intended to be achieved a small fee is owed, invested by the dreamer, when parents want their children to go to college to study they should help them, and in this way both can realize their dreams.

Dreams are made easier when we pay a small fee. Do not give up on your dreams, stay active and on top of them so that they become a reality. Be determined to find the best way to achieve your goals, but if by chance of life, things do not go the way you have imagined and dreamed. If it does not come out as expected, do not fall into despair. Do not stop your attempt; do not give rise to depression. Those who fail to achieve what they seek it's because their persistence and continuous work has weaken, they retire once they are presented with the first setback on the road, however the drawbacks are part of the process to be exhausted, the obstacles serve as steps to climb, it is not possible to jump on a ladder from one rung to another one that is higher, the fall could be dangerous and harmful for the one who tries such a feat, you must go up step by step until you reach the end, step by step. If the instance you try to go up one by one until you reach the last and still slide down.

The next action is to start over again with the same enthusiasm as at first, if you knew someone who has never failed is because that person has not tried anything, failures are part of life itself, if not, observe a child when it begins to walk. He falls, gets up, rises until he manages to walk to perfection, it's the same when people undertake a new project, chances are that at the beginning, perhaps, they do not achieve the desired fruit but after time, he who has preserved without fainting will succeed in successfully harvesting the result of all their effort, care, constancy and perseverance.

If you cannot realize your dreams in the time and the moment you dreamed, that is no reason to give up or get discouraged, you can still achieve even if you have to wait a little longer, do not stop dreaming for fear of failure, keep trying, you are as intelligent as any other person on earth, you possess aptitudes, believe that it is the best thing that can do for yourself and for others, each one of us can realize a multitude of activities, that can take you to triumph and to become a person of great success, do not leave your dreams in abandonment, keep them afloat.

Your talents could remain like a beautiful pearl inside its shell, remaining as a pearl, but enclosed you will never be able to adorn the beautiful neck of a fine and elegant woman, you need to come out so that together with others you can form a beautiful necklace or beautiful earrings, in addition no one would know that the pearl is part of the universe, it will be unknown, but if it comes out, not only will it highlight the beauty of a lady it will also achieve the dream of being in an exotic showcase on display, so that the public has the opportunity to admire it, yet if not purchasing it.

Do not give up on your dreams, there is no greater happiness than being able to see them fulfilled, it will bring you, and yours, and your community enormous joy.

If you find discouraging people who tell you that you will not succeed do not listen to their comments, be courageous; do not pay attention to those who say you cannot do it; you always can, if you put your heart in what you want to achieve, continue with your dreams even if they seem small, or if they seem impossible in the eyes of others, do not let yourself be intimidate, do not allow your right to dream to be stolen, the dreams may be small but at their right time they could become giants.

The only drawback when you want to achieve a dream is that it is not achieved by magic, it is not a matter of luck, I believe in luck accompanied by action, and a good preparation is essential, obligatory, and basic for the doors to open in any stage of life. To obtain whatever the dream that it may be, the investment is necessary, the bigger the dream that is wanted, the greater amount of energy it requires, decision and almost all require a certain amount of money, everything will depend on what the dream is, what is aspired to become or have. If you want to be the best runner in the world, there are many resources that you will have to invest and you must train every day, maintain an adequate diet, and ensure to take time to rest and a number of other requirements that is essential to fulfill your dream of being the best runner in the world.

If you stop to think that running is pointless, or that there already are many runners, that are faster than you, you can be sure that things will take another course.

Dreams are achieved with a positive attitude, sufficient dedication, hard work and therefore a great deal of persistence, in addition to other conditions that must be applied to be able to succeed in everything you undertake.

A dream will never be too small, nor less important than another, even large corporations started from a simple idea, which with attention, effort, care, perseverance and continued work, have become the giants they are today.

Do not give up on your dreams.

Do not give up on your dreams

D o not give up on your dreams, on the treasures of this world, everyone regardless of race, nationality or creed, we all have rights, and we own them.

If the mountain you climb is very high, put stone on stone, do not stop working if any of them fall, do not think twice about it begin again.

Never perceive yourself to be small; even when you fail in your endeavors, he who has not failed has not attempted anything. Insist, dream, one day you will make it.

Conquer your dreams

The great conquerors of the past and those who have succeeded today, have broken all barriers, reaching out-of-bounds limits.

Those of yesterday and today have passed their own expectations, achieved spectacular results, so great that even today, we benefit from their incredible feats; it is very likely that they have had to break ground.

Where there was not the slightest chance that a life could survive, however, they not only succeeded in surviving, they have left their legacies for all humanity. Sometimes some people, although they have dreams, fail to realize them, not because they lack potential or talent, rather because they let themselves be influenced by an unfavorable environment, which teaches them since childhood to be losers, per se, not that it is good or bad to teach children that much is earned as it can also be lost. Losing, gives them the tools for later when things are not going well, teaches them to get back up, and that a failure in what they initiate, could later become the anchor that sustains them, and for that reason it would make it easier to start up again.

Another problem that is also not favorable is that some adults, without thinking about the damage they cause in the minds of minors, those who have not yet matured enough to overcome the labels put on them by some adults, labeling them with words and phrases, defeatist.

Instead of encouraging them to continue ahead, to let them know that it is possible, often people reach adulthood thinking that their dreams are impossible to conquer; dear friend if this has been your case, I want you to know that you can do it, get out there and conquer what you have much dreamed of, I also do not want you to forget that: numerous amounts of people around the world have had the courage, the rage, and enough audacity to overcome the difficulties and or miss steps that they have had to endure.

All of them as great conquerors have not let themselves be defeated; on the contrary they have been winners. You, just like all those brave people, you are a winner, think, get up, keep going, whatever you want, you can achieve.

Others despite not having a mentor, a guide or a person to show them the way to go.

They have taken a small seed, which has been their banner, their desire to succeed, alone, without help from anyone have transcended all borders.

They have surprised the world, as the sun in its full splendor have shone with their own light, and in sum to their great deeds, have stood at the height of the stars.

That gap that these people have opened where there was not even the smallest and remote possibility of achievement and triumph. Human beings like each one of us with an idea sown in our mind, gave it maintenance and put it to work, when there were no signs that the idea could germinate, and if by chance they were to ask life for an opinion, the answer would be that the idea would not bare good results, due to lack of value. Whatever your idea, your little seed, that which, apparently, and before the eyes of others, would not germinate even if it were planted in good and fertile soil, but with the proper care you, my dear reader, can bring to the surface that conqueror within.

In life there will always be as many difficulties as possibilities, overcome the first ones and go in search of the second ones, realize your dream do not let it get away from your hands, as long as you are still alive there is time; while you can breathe there is opportunity to succeed.

Put your mind and hands to work.

The triumphs are for those who dare to go through the world conquering their dreams, the obstacles are many, but without them we would never know that we have overcome, far from the problems that present themselves in people's lives, nobody would be able to enjoy the happiness of having worked with great determination, and that one is a strong human being, able to overcome the fences, the walls and obstacles that in one form or another each one of us has to face, although each one of us in a different way.

Once having defeated and all those traps that appear on the road have been pulled down, then it can be confirmed that you have conquered your triumphs.

Give your life meaning

Many difficulties arise in the life of a person over the years, but there are millions who do not allow adverse situations to undermine their existences, there are people, who have decided, to give their lives meaning, independently of the problem they might be going through.

Some have transgressed diseases, suffering, anguish, pain, physical abuse, and psychological, among other harsh realities, that some human beings face or have been forced to endure, against their will circumstances that sadden the soul, and in some cases, lowers self-esteem.

Others in turn have not allowed problems to intimidate them, on the contrary, they have decided to make a change in their reality by giving their lives meaning, because they know that they are valuable and that while they are alive all the hopes exist of being able to move forward, embarking on a new path that leads them to realize unimaginable dreams, because they know that life is the most valuable treasure that a person can have.

The mere fact of existing, is reason enough to smile, living is a privilege that we all must value, and at the same time know that all human beings came to the world with an immense ability to succeed in any situation they have to face, whatever the situation that they have been through or is happening to them at that moment in their life, do not let yourself be frightened, do not be sad, smile at life, do not suffer for what has no solution, but if there is the possibility that there may be one, do not just cross your arms, fight, advance, you are a valuable being, there is nothing more valuable in the world than a person.

Stop a little in front of a mirror; look at what a beautiful person you are, or have you not realized that you have more qualities than flaws? If it is nighttime, enjoy the brightness of the stars, if it is day time feel the splendor of the sun, enjoy the smell of the flowers in spring, when they blossom they are happy and smiley. Have you heard the trill of the birds? Every break of dawn they sing, and they never complain.

Have you ever observed the butterflies, they are happy when they flutter over the roses; they do not stop to think about their short existence. They enjoy the nectar, as if they were to live forever. Give your life meaning, and remember that people are important, for the simple fact, of that of being a person.

People are worth because they are human beings, not for what they have or do not have, but he, who intends to achieve a dream in their life, has all the opportunity in the world.

Cultivate the love for yourself, and for the other people of the planet, and for all the creatures of the universe, without going to the extreme. We are all here, in this ship called the world with a purpose, to be happy and yes, to allow others to be happy as well. Give your life meaning.

Do not let anyone stop you, go in search of your dreams

Every day thousands and millions of people in the world, since their childhood they listen to an adult, they even listen to their own parents, grandparents, uncles, brothers, neighbors, friends of the family and some teachers, who have been putting labels on them since their early years. They tell the children you are going to be this or that when you grow up, where clearly in most cases minimizing the will force, the character, and personality of the child.

Ignoring the intelligence that each person has within them, they carry in their genes. Rather forgetting that those who are children today will be adults tomorrow, without those little boys and girls, the towns, communities, countries and the world in general will cease to exist. Without children there would be no future, no nation or country.

If you mistreat children with words or deeds, you will one day in your life grow to regret it, because those children once they become adults will have control of our countries, children today by natural law of life will be the future rulers, doctors, farmers, lawyers, technicians and guardians of that beautiful country where you and those children live. It is unfair to label children.

And even worse is to tell them that they are of no use, that speech should be changed, they should be encouraged to succeed, tell them that everything is possible, and that they are intelligent, since they are small or since much earlier, from the womb, to make them feel important and safe, not minimize them.

It is not right to compare within one or another sibling, or neighbor, or cousin, etc.

We would have fewer problems in the world, if we would tell the children that they are each good and intelligent; that the future is theirs and to not stop dreaming, that children can too dream, that by studying, working, and doing the right things one can live better.

We must guide the children to grow to be men and women of good, to be able to offer society, and the homeland worthy people. When children receive a good family education, and are urged to study for sure they will have a better future.

When you have a dream whatever it may be, do not let anyone put a break on your dreams by allowing them tell you that you cannot do it, that there will be much inconvenience on the way, just close your eyes, and cover your ears, do not listen to those pessimistic voices that want to stop you, go ahead, walk, run, go in search of your dreams, do not stop, the route can be extensive, but there is no road that can go for long that seems to have no end. Arm yourself with courage, strength, rage, audacity, boldness do not let others choose for you, do not let anyone in this world extinguish that fire that you have in your heart, that heat that burns within you, that desire to succeed, you know what you want, get over the obstacles.

It is known that to reach a star, there is much to climb, but above what other people can tell you that you cannot do it, but for he who fights can accomplish anything, dreams can be achieved.

Do not let anyone stop you, go in search of your dreams. It is certain that in life on the way towards the goal, one will find some limitations, some that will try to oppose it, to stand in the way so that you cannot keep ahead, to those people who put rocks and all type of barriers in your way, telling you that you cannot do it, that will not give you anything for what you need, that you must choose something easier, that that is not for your type of person, as long as things are done right according to earthly and divine laws.

Everything is possible. Put all your effort, so that in the end that idea, that dream that only belongs to you, becomes a reality, do not admit to the discouragers in your life, or their ideas, do not let yourself be frightened by the stumbling blocks of the sidewalk, if you cannot find the path made, start working to thresh a new path, in the end you will have conquered what you have so much dreamed of.

Discover your dreams

If you have not yet discovered your dream, in case you have not experienced that awakening that some people have, if you do not know or are not sure what you want to do in life, it is time to discover your dreams, I am not referring to the dreams that you have while you are asleep, no, is to dream when you are awake, with all the beautiful, wonderful things that the universe has to offer and that they belong to you by divine order.

All that you can do and build with your ideas and your efforts, to taste it, to believe that you can do it and that the impossible becomes reality. Imagine that someone wants to plant a tree in the front lawn or the back yard of their house, the first step will be to investigate if they reproduce by seed or planting a twig, you should find the right way to plant it, take care of it, that is already a small effort, this tree in a prudent time will grow, but it is not enough to sow it and leave it there to grow abandoned, the sower must not forget that the tree requires love and patience to have a healthy development, care and a waiting time are necessary.

Because a tree does not grow overnight, its growth time will depend on the type of tree it is, and if you want it to give fruit, the more fruits you want it to produce, the greater the waiting time. As in the instance of a tree it poses a similarity to the dreams that a person wants to achieve, the first thing is to find out what their dream is, because each person wants to achieve to be or do different things, find out what your dream is that is if you do not yet know what yours is.

Remember that the good and interesting things in life require constancy, concentration and a great deal of love and dedication, once you discover it, pay attention to it, because if you neglect it you could get stuck floating in midair, it would end up in the list of the unfulfilled dreams, that way it would never give the desired fruits, in case your dream is to be president, a doctor, a painter, a good laborer, or an excellent housewife.

To climb a mountain or to be the best football player, a robot builder, or choose one of those technical careers that are so necessary, continue do not stop; keep ahead pursue your dream. Imagine that someone wants to be a good farmer or a day laborer, of the many that every day get up very early in the morning to sow the fruits of their labor, the legumes, the fruits and vegetables which at a worldwide level everyone places on their tables.

The first thing that we must take into account is that it is a beautiful work, to realize one should have a heart full of love, will, enthusiasm.

It is difficult work, hard, beautiful, delicate, in case nobody wants to sow what would become of mankind, someone might think that no one would dear dream of a job as a farmer, it's one of the most dignified trades that there is, if there were no dedicated day laborers, with that love that springs from the depths of their heart, most people would die worldwide. It is one of the most beautiful yet exhausting jobs.

In short what I mean to say is, that whatever your dream is, it is important and valuable.

No dream is too large for you to reach, nor too small for someone to just minimize.

Everything is important and necessary at the same time, everything good that is realized with the thought of others or of humanity in mind, will have a place of prestige in society.

When it's about discovering and realizing a dream one must take into account what legacy we will leave future generations. And above all, that it's not only for personal gain, but also for the benefit of all. Centuries after centuries and through the years we have been witness to the dreams that different people have accomplished, perhaps it took sleepless nights, restless hours, but today all humanity benefits from the achievements and dreams reached by those people who are no longer here, however their dreams have immortalized them, to discover a dream there is no age limit, it's always possible, as long as there is life and breathe, all possibilities are in your favor, opportunities will always be waiting for those who have desire to succeed, going after your dream the only thing you are doing to yourself is to help prolong your life, because your brain will be full of energy, as a result of that motivation you have, that energy will become a bit more of life source for that person, I have met people in their 20's with less motivation and energy than one in their 80's, that means that a good motivation, could help achieve a resounding change in the life of a person.

My father has told me that my great-grandfather, a hundred years old, was in search of employment and when my grandfather questioned him about such idea, he replied that he had the strength to work and he did not want anyone to keep him from that. It does not matter in which corner of the planet each person is at, whether you have schooling or not, ideas arise from intelligence, that lady is brought from the factory, you are intelligent, like most people.

Each and every human being possesses his or her own wisdom; intelligence is as diverse as a person is. All human beings have the potential, which allows them to perform, a task, a labor or function to make their dreams come true. Find out where your potential lies and what your skills are. Surely you will be surprised, when you discover all the things you can achieve.

If you cannot go in a hurry, then go slowly.

It seems that the things we dream to achieve, at first glance they appear so distant or difficult to achieve, they seem so far away that they could be believed or seem to be unreachable before the human eye, it could be the case that someone may want to climb a high mountain, so sublime and majestic that one could not even think that any one person would be daring enough to climb it, even one of the most trained climbers would think twice before daring to challenge a plateau of such great magnitude.

It is very likely that you cannot climb with the ease of a flying eagle, but if you try there are millions of possibilities to overcome the obstacles, and reach the highest part of the top. Most of the things one wants to achieve require time, dedication, efforts, and above all, a great deal of braveness.

If you observe the calm, determination, boldness, fortitude and bravery of a river, it seldom is in a hurry, except when there has been a lot of rain fall, but in spite of all that amount of water it carries it does not stop, not for a single second, never backsliding, has an iron determination, a fixed point to which it wants to arrive to with its torrent or calm waters, sometimes so calm that they seem immobile with its serenity and moderation, but always deciding to reach its destination.

When you make the decision to reach a goal, follow the example of the river, never stopping, if you cannot go in a hurry, with the momentum and speed that the wind carries, breathe do as the river does, go slowly, never look back when achieving a purpose is all that it is about, value, constancy, integrity, persistence, tenacity and effective work, will take you to the top.

In case you do not see immediate results, do not faint, keep ahead, do not waste time with laments, for the setbacks in the road, they almost always serve as stairs and support, they push you to reach the place of interest and achieve all things beautiful and wonderful that every human being deserves by divine order, but remember that even so, to reach the goal, investment is necessary, at least a little imagination, enthusiasm, faith, hope, a touch of joy, even if things do not seem possible at that given moment, smile, to be happy in the midst of turbulence can heal the soul, eliminating sadness is one of the most important medicines, when achieving something is all that it is about. If you cannot go in a hurry go slowly, but get out there...

Passing across the river

It is very difficult to pass to the other side of the river, when its waters are deep. Even though it's crystal clear waters have nothing to envy from the great blue sky. And what to say when it bears the implacable fury of a hurricane or when it has so many turbulent and dirty waters, razing with everything in its path, who would dare to cross a river that does not hear the clamor of the trees, nor the song of the birds asking it to slow down and regain its composure, it seems impossible to cross to the other side of the river in adverse circumstances, even more so when it continues steadily in its path not listening, and ignoring everything that happens around it, it becomes an uphill journey crossing through any river, in those conditions however small the river may be.

Nevertheless thousands of people in the world have had to wait for the water currents in their lives to have calmed down, to be able to keep ahead with their objective. Everything can be obtained despite sometimes having to wait, and in spite of the difficulties, it is necessary to try and cross, we all know that some people have had to cross to the other side of the river defying all the problems that they have encountered in their trajectory through this world, but as humans they have adapted to any situation surpassing all the challenges with exceedingly fortitude, without giving way neither to sadness nor to discouragement, it is true that the problems of life weakens some of them while it makes others stronger to continue fighting and working in order to cross to the other side of the river.

You who have a dream and are on the opposite side of the river, if your waters carry the fury of a volcano, do not be discouraged; wait a little longer, when everything is calm, try to continue, keep dreaming, everything is possible, think a little, even the stones and debris that the river drags could serve as a bridge to cross to the other side, and thus acquire the desired ending, of course crossing to the other side of the river is a metaphor, each person one way or another has had to arm themselves with faith, strength and courage to be able to defeat all the barriers encountered on their journey on this ship called world and to cross to the other side.

Crossing the desert

A desert is an uninhabited, uninhabited where there are no people, devoid of vegetation due to lack of rain, sandy or stony, is a place where its only inhabitants could be scorpions, lizards, snakes and perhaps some cacti. Trying to cross it could become an odyssey, because in it does not exist the minimal possibility of life, any human being who will dare try crossing it, would be signing his death sentence, not all people as brave as they are would dare to make such a dangerous feat in every sense of the word.

However, thousands of people in the world have had to take strength from where there is none. Because the desert they have had to cross in their lives has been far more valid, desolate and inhospitable, whose sand dunes do not differ from those that can only be found in the different deserts of the world.

Whatever your desert, try to cross it, do not be afraid of the challenges, you must overcome, from the pitfalls and obstacles of a desert, in one way or another all the people one can see triumphant and successful, have had to cross not one but several and great deserts in their lives, for today you, I, and all of us can see them shining like the stars, and high, as if they had never been on the first rung of the ladder, or on the ground, because in one way or another, to ascend to heaven, one must first be on the ground, no one can climb, if one was not once under. Difficult task and almost impossible to defy is the quicksand that in the deserts pushes the winds.

All human beings have a level of adaptation to overcome, however difficult the road may seem, and no matter how infinite it may be, whoever has determination, fortitude, persistence, faith, hope, which must never be lost, are capable not only of crossing the immense and dangerous deserts, but to go much further in order to reach the dream that you have waited for your whole life. In order for dreams to be fulfilled, it is necessary for the people to make a commitment to himself, to commit to themselves to pursue without stopping in search of that desired dream.

Your idea might be so small that it would seem that it would never grow, perhaps as a grain of sand of the millions and millions that form the sand dunes, if you stop and think for a bit, your tiny idea has all the possibilities to become a powerful and giant ship that will allow you to cross the desert without letting the drought affect you, and not let yourself be blinded by the sands that the winds carry.

Do not let the cactus with its thorns stop you, continue joining forces, when you want to realize a dream, you must move forward, to let yourself be discouraged by everything that you find on the road is useless, because it leads nowhere, however difficult things get It is necessary to continue with motivation, and great desire to continue steadily is one of the most important tools when it comes to walking along a long path, if you stop for fear of the scorpions, snakes and lizards of the desert, you will never reach the desired goal.

The most appropriate thing to do in this case would be to obviate it if you can but if you cannot just keep going, in any case there will be no road there, it is your responsibility, because in the event that someone before you have passed through that same place the sand would have already erased the path, so you would have to trace your own way.

In case exhaustion, fatigue, stress, and pain in your feet want to hold you back, relax for a few seconds, and rest for a moment, it is necessary for good health. But do not sleep too much, you could fall into apathy, leisure is one of the worst enemies when you want to reach a destination, that dream for which you have waited and worked so hard for requires good and positive energies.

Dare to cross the desert of life; take advantage of the warmth and energy of the desert, proceed forward with giant steps, with fervor, determination, enthusiasm, life is beautiful, even if it is accompanied by all those adverse and difficult desert situations. Cross the desert of life, in the end you will have the satisfaction of having achieved it. You can do it; there is no limit to it, when you want to achieve your dreams.

Only you have the power to achieve your dreams

Many people have dreams, goals, purposes, objectives, which they would like to achieve, but doubt embarrasses them and dare not ask for opinions from others, many encourage them to continue ahead and try to do it because it might yield good results, however others less optimistic, who tells them that this or that thing will not succeed. Thousands of times we have heard discouraging people, who tell young people who have the desire and hope of becoming a doctor, lawyer, engineer, artist, painter, singer or any other profession or trade, say to them that there are already many in that profession and that this or that trade does not make money, and that it is a waste of time, in the case of artists, actresses and actors even tell them that they have no talent, leave that and start doing something else that will yield more money.

All those bad recommendations are not true, for the simple reason that each person, besides having the right to make it work and to dream with what their heart desires, as long as it is not detrimental to others, one should not allow to be influenced, by those who say that there is already a lot of them, but even if there is, it will never be too much for someone to give up dreaming.

There will always be a need for, more companies, more people prepared in the different areas that exist, be they technical, superior, diligent hands and ready to work will never be irrelevant, more and more dreamers are needed in the world every day and minute that elapses, because every day more people are born and there are more living beings on the planet who are dependent of those dreamers. Thanks to God and to all those dreamers who have existed and exist it's the reason that the world keeps on moving, dreams accompanied by good studies are the basis to be able to guarantee a better and greater quality of life for the dreamer and those in their lives, and even for society in general, because thanks to all who have persevered in their dreams today we can benefit from the technology, with all its advances, and all the vitally important things that scientists in different areas have bequeathed to us worldwide.

Those people who never paid attention to those disheartening who unscrupulously told them that project or that idea would not work. Those people who ignored the comments of others, kept ahead with more faith, and continued their intention and project of life, and left us all their events and research in medicine, chemistry, literature, art and what to say of those who dreamed of uniting the world by means of airplanes, ships, automobiles, or those who dreamed of going to the moon, things that seemed surreal and that without a doubt are a gigantic reality.

They were certain that their ideas were good, they believed in themselves, in the good results they expected from their dreams, and in the end their aspirations carried them from triumph to triumph and from glory to glory. Only you have the power to achieve your dreams. Do not let anyone stop you, only the brave who do not fear difficulties, those who are capable of overcoming obstacles and inconveniences, have the will and the power to get ahead in everything they undertake.

Only you have the power to achieve your dreams.

Commit to your dream

From childhood we observe how two people who love each other make great commitments to keep respect, to love each other, and to be together for life, sometimes they are only verbal commitments because people who love themselves with purity do not require papers for their love to have validity.

Others make a pact where the parties are committed to take care of the company and work to grow it, and develop it in such a way that they acquire greater benefits for all involved.

Some are committed to keep secret from other people. All those agreements and commitments each different in their own way but of great importance for those who have to execute it. When people make an agreement with another, they have a great responsibility to comply with this agreement, even if it was not written, verbally, today almost all agreements are made in writing, because things have changed, the world and some people, commit, but do not comply.

In past times there was no difference whether it was verbal or written, both parties fulfilled with the word pledged, just as in the past people are thirsty and desire to achieve some things that are of benefit to them, their families and society.

You, just as everyone else, have a dream, if it has not yet become reality, if you already know what it is, once you have managed to identify it or that goal with which you have begun to dream. There remains an arduous task, to make a covenant, with yourself, to make that dream come true.

Stop, observe, think, analyze.

If your dream is one of those that require time, or if you can simply get it in a shorter time, you will know that if it is going long, you need to prepare your mind, not to fall into apathy, and despair, a longer term project needs more dedication, greater enthusiasm, interest, motivation, and sufficient energy, so that one does not want to abandon it in the first setback that appears on the journey, or the first difficulty, because, although it may seem strange; it's all part of the process. Commitment to one is something serious, because it requires of a good dose of encouragement, positive thinking, your time, maybe hours without sleep, without rest, to work with courage and constancy and above all to lose the fear of failure, it is impossible to fail on your first attempt for those reasons known or unknown, but that is no reason to be discouraged even when the winds do not blow in his favor.

If you have already made a commitment to yourself to move forward even in the darkness of the night, that same agreement, will impel you to lose the fear, and to embark on the conquest of the desired treasure, that with which you have dreamed of so much.

Commitment means that some things will have to be put aside to give all your attention to that purpose that will definitely lead you to the top of the mountain, whatever your own may be continue climbing, at the end joy and happiness will invade you due to the triumph reached.

If you have a dream but you spend more time sleeping, watching TV, or other things that distract you from the goal, it is not that you are not going to get what you want, the time just has to be put in. In having it, because a project that is what it mostly requires that you devote time to it. Stripping yourself of the debris on the road that keeps you from continuing, that forms part of the commitment made with yourself, to obtain the doorway that that dream has always longed for. Imagine a track and field runner who dreams of achieving a gold or silver medal at the Olympic Games, but is neglectful in their training and diet, knowing that there will be other competitors from around the world, who are likely to have trained enough to win it, if this person who wants the medal whichever one, does not dedicate the required time and necessary care, you will never be able to achieve the desired dream, but in your case, remember that there are no other competitors, the commitment is with yourself, because it is personal, in this case you will need a greater effort on your part, a good preparation in whatever area, whatever your dream, the star you want to reach, your goal, your goal is essential work, patience, and dedication, to use the power of the mind as a driving force, to commit to what you want so much, and above all to know and have the security, faith, and certainty that he who dedicates efforts, time, to any work, company, activity, occupation the results will be favorable, they will be optimal.

Then commit yourself to your dream.

Dare to dream

Fear could become a double-edged sword at any certain moment, but depending on the circumstance it is favorable, and of a great power, because a little fear, at one point could serve to protect your life and that of others.

I imagined that you are a good driver, who is guiding your vehicle, you comply with all traffic rules established by law, you drive under the speed limit, indicated on the tracks, through which you drive on, you stop where it says to stop, including at traffic lights as it is needed, you slow down at intersections.

All this to be able to maintain the privilege of driving and traveling on the roads with a vehicle, but also because you are a bit scared, hitting or causing a traffic accident or hurting yourself or others, this is the type of fear that protects your life and that of others, who have the same right to travel the roads.

Assuming that there is bad weather and they announce to all the people not leave their homes because there is flooding danger, if the citizens hear the call of the authorities, and they do not leave their homes, for the fear that something bad might happen to them, or that the bad weather might trap them, or when they tell those who travel on the high seas, to they not go out, because the waves are furious, in case no one leaves their homes fulfilling the mandates for fear of the worse waters; that fear without any doubt is protective.

But if it is about an inner fear, to fail, fear of not being able to obtain or move forward in a project, if you do not set start to your dream because you think it will not have the expected results, it is time to dare to dream aside from fear of failure, you should never stop doing something for fear that it will not work, how would one know if it will give optimal results, if you do not start.

Think about how you will achieve, see the stars in your hands, as high as they might be, losing your fear is a very important step to go in search of your dreams, to cast aside the fear of failure in one of the greatest feats that a human being possesses when it comes to reaching a dream, intimidation leads to no way out, breaking the chains of fear and disinterest is the main dish in the menu of dreams.

Advance, continue without fainting, do not forget that your priority and commitment must be to achieve success in the area of your interest; your merits and your achievements depend on the commitment you create.

And with everything you want to achieve. You are the star and the stars are yours.

DARE TO DREAM.

Only you have the power to achieve what you want

If ever in your life you have thought that only those who have lots of money and those who hold the power of the countries in the different nations in the world are the only ones who can dream of achieving great triumphs and get all the beautiful and valuable things, in material, intellectual and spiritual terms that exists in the universe.

You are thinking in a closed minded manner, because although it seems strange and distant, you who at this moment has taken a little of your time to read my humble notes, which I have written just for the purpose of motivating you and someone else to keep ahead, do not faint even if the strong storms are whipping without mercy, you who thinks that your dreams can not come true, there is always an opportunity for you and for all the people who have had the privilege of being in this small boat called the world or however somebody wants to call it, the truth is that we are all here without exception, and as long as we abstain from that wonderful and great privilege of being alive, we must not stop dreaming, because the dreams themselves serve as medicine to cure even the deepest of wounds or the worse of diseases.

It is true that many have purchasing power, others power of decisions, and a series of powers that I would never finish mentioning them all because the list is immense. Just like them, people that neither you nor I know, and maybe we do not know they exist, and they also do not know anything about you, me, or other people who are anonymous because we are not in the eye of the media.

The fact that we are not public or political figures does not mean that you cannot dream and achieve great things, and realize the dream of your life. Only you have the power through your thought, your creation, your decision and your preparation for your dream to be fulfilled.

Not by magic.

Iam not the type of person, who believes that things are achieved by the art of magic, but if you believe, it is your right and I respect it, but I urge you to add the following ingredients mentioned above, idea, creation, decision and above all a good dose of preparation and dedication, with all of that the results will be optimal.

The power of positive thinking, constancy, and freedom that provides a vast preparation in the area that you like and suits you, study is likely to not guarantee success at a particular time, but will surely open the doors even when you least expect it, in case you do not like it:

* If you cannot study, do not be discouraged there are a series of achievements and opportunities in the universe.

* That does not require studies, I know that the circumstances of each individual are different; dreams are diverse and immense, dream with what you want, many opportunities of triumph there are on the planet, start yours and you will see how.

* The universe becomes on your favor by pouring all its good energies towards you.

* Make sure your dream, if it does not favor someone it at least will not harm them, everyone has the right to.

* Do and be what they want, everyone is free to do what they want as long as their freedom does not affect.

* Other living beings. The power to achieve that which you so much desire is in you in your mind.

* In your interior, do not let that force that is inside you escape without you having achieved.

* The dream of your life. Only you have the power to achieve what you want.

Draw strength to continue, even if you draw it from the soles of your feet

In the olden times when carriages did not exist; carts, donkeys, horses and camels were perhaps destined for a much reduced and very small group that for whatever the reason had the ability to have one.

When science had not yet reached that preponderant place that today is seen in almost the whole world, for the simple reason that there are very few corners where science has not arrived with its positive advances, in its different rolls. The magnitude of how far science can reach an unprecedented event, for the benefit of all humanity.

All these advances that we have today, in past and remote times did not exist, however most people on the planet did not stop for lack of technology, and all those wonders that we enjoy now.

Almost everyone was obligated to have to be on foot when they wanted to move from one place to another. They walked long paths, they crossed mountains, rivers, brooks, and they had to go a long distance on foot. They crossed paths so distant that no one could imagine they would be tired, worn, exhausted but always firm because they had a goal, to someday reach that place that for many it was only a dream.

Whole days and nights walking in the middle of the darkness and under the hot sun, in most cases there was no road, they had carve it in order to keep going, nevertheless they did not faint they continued with their trajectory despite the conditions to reach the goal were not the most propitious, however as much as they walked and tried to reach the road it became increasingly remote, measured and hostile, sometimes cold, and other times rugged and dry, where you could not even see the minimal possibility that one could reach the desired goal. But they never gave up, their persistence.

Perhaps a little obstinacy pushed them to continue, barefoot, with injured feet, muddy or dusty, with the dirt or sand from the road, nothing and no one stopped them with a hard decision, with the strength of their mind, with a heart ready to continue even in the midst of pain, and exhausting fatigue.

Because of the harshness of the journey, their end had an end that was important for them and for theirs, they sought strength and courage from where there was none to reach the place of their destiny, and thus to obtain the final goal. They never gave up, did not stop, they continued with a fierce decision despite the setbacks and battles, perhaps, not the way, many did not find it and had to carve it when walking. Now days where we live we are blessed, science and technology have advanced in a gigantic way, it seems easier for people to give up their efforts to obtain their dreams, they even lose enthusiasm, motivation, some set off and then abandon their project, at the first site of a stone in their shoe, they lose hope and even a little faith, in their own self and see what they want to achieve be very far away.

Dear reader, I hope this is neither your story nor your case, but in case your strength is diminishing, it is time to get to your feet, time to get up, to make your way through the path of life that only belongs to you and no one else, to travel, to draw strength from where there is none, to get it from the soles of your feet, they possess an irresistible force, ask your feet how is it that they can withstand all the weight of your body, I have already asked mine and I have followed their example, they never complain of the weight of the body, even when tired and worn and exhausted, they continue walking until arriving at its final destination. If you feel weak due to everyday problems: look at your feet, watch them carefully, do not let yourself be overwhelmed, do not put sadness in your heart, tell your mind that it is strong.

Keep ahead like the people of those ancient times who walked, though already knowing that their goal was far, once a decision was made hey would not stop until arriving. If you feel that you can no longer take strength from the soles of your feet if necessary, only those who struggle incessantly, without stopping carrying all the weight that life has given them, they have the opportunity and the joy of being able to say it was difficult, but I have succeeded. I have been crowned; I have the bliss of the expected dream.

Begin, continue, and never give up

All the beginnings of any task, work, project, at the beginning could be very difficult especially for a novel, for a person who starts practicing an art, profession or any trade, business or task, it will be difficult, complicated. Making certain choices is an uphill for those who want and have the desire to achieve or reach a goal. For those who have not tried anything once before it could be frightening at first, however it will be easier if you cover yourself with a breastplate that is called strength.

Sister of courage can begin to put stones, on top of stones, without realizing soon you will have a mountain of them, the same person will wonder how some can be put on top of the others and all in order, however, if instead one starts to think about the time that it will take to place them, one on top of another, it will take longer.

In case you feel that you have not obtained the expected results and with the urgency initially thought, giving up, leaving your dreams aside, neglecting the actions that would take you to climb your own mountain, giving up in a world so competitive is not a good option, would be like throwing himself into the void without a parachute, where falling and the hard impact on the ground would be imminent, sinking into discouragement, only serves as an impediment when the intent is to finish the job. It is like being stranded in the middle of the road because of lack of fuel, energy is needed to be able to continue in the attempt to ascend to the highest mountain, to be over taken, to no avail, if the conditions do not give themselves and the fury of the storm is hitting them hard, they must continue anyway, it is possible that where they have tried to enter, everything has been closed, if the doors are closed and the path is not yet carved, your duty and obligation is to do carve it.

Even through the middle of the interwoven trees and molasses, do not wait for someone else to do it for you in order for you to pass through, allow others to walk through yours, you will surely have a greater satisfaction, at the end of the journey, your soul and your heart will be filled with joy at the thought that that vast road was made by your own hands, that you are the architect and builder of such a valuable project. Start, trace path to where there is none.

Continue never give up.

Put on the armor of a warrior

In ancient times, many men went to war to wage great battles to defend their homeland, their country, their family, they all had something in common, no one was going to face a battle with the simple garments they wore, to carry out the daily tasks of a citizen, they would put on their armor, a kind of iron or metal clothing, in order to protect themselves from the darts and bullets of their enemies, they wore helmets; they used to protect their arms, hands, feet and their entire body, now days these heavy garments are no longer used. All this is part of history.

Every person who lives on this planet earth, in one way or another from time to time face small and great battles, as a warrior there are many difficulties and stumbling blocks that have to be fought, some people, every day experience situations as in a place of combat. Many of those battles leave wounds and lacerations in the soul, and because they are hidden wounds they are not easy to heal. Prepare yourself for when these battles come, from which no one is excluded from, because all human beings are faced with problems that sometimes are out of the control.

Put on the armor of a warrior so you can protect yourself from the poisoned darts, for they are like the variables in an experiment where there are some that are definitely impossible to control. The clashes and difficult situations that many people go through become uncontrollable, as they are unavoidable it is necessary to put on the armor of a warrior to be able to appear at the front of the battle, the more problems and difficulties that are destined, do not stop when the fire is on, when the flames are more ardent and everything appears that it will be destroyed, it is there when you are near victory, do not withdraw in the middle of the battle, be sure to wear the armor of the warrior, keep fighting, this world is for the courageous, for those who turn the challenges into valuable opportunities. Whatever your battle; illness, loneliness, separation, if you are missing something, continue fighting, do not faint, do not stop, exude the strength and courage of the great warriors. Once his armor is on, a warrior shows his bravery, strength, and rage needed to be at the forefront of the battle, whatever your battle do not abandon it, remember that a good warrior never leaves the place of combat until they finish what they started. In your case everything will depend on how strong is your ability to fight, victory is not for those who withdraw leaving the battlefield, and the crown is for the risk takers. Put on the armor of a warrior.

Where there is ash imagine a ladder

A long time ago a lady approached me and told me a story, she told me that she had no house, that she lived in a hotel, because her house, a house that had cost her a lot of money and sacrifice, because she had worked very hard for 35 years to buy it and pay for it, a house in a high middle class neighborhood, for her very expensive. One Christmas day her family left town for another family member's home, but someone had left a heater on and that caused a fire to burn her house down, and that left all her belongings and her house in ashes, just imagining about the impact she would feel when arriving and not finding anything of what had been her home just gave me chills, because no one imagines going out to visit someone and when they get back and see all their efforts, sacrifices and money turned to ash.

She was sad and distraught, when she spoke with me it had already been several months since that sad event, no matter how positive someone is, one will suffer for something like what happened to her, but thank God that at least at the time of the event no one was home, there was no human loss. Even though the house insurance paid for the hotel and she was going to buy another house, even then sadness still engulfed her, because all her documents and personal belongings had been burned, everything was left in ashes. Anyone who was in the situation of the lady, would crumble, could be caught by the anguish, sadness and grief; because losing everything that has been built through sweat and sometimes even tears is not easy or flattering. Losing everything all of a sudden without knowing where to go, however brave and strong the person, it would cause a series of psychological effects, anxiety, stress, depression and other symptoms caused by extreme situations. The distinguished lady did not know me, nor I her. We happened to be in a public place, and without knowing whom I was, she wanted to tell me what had happened to her. She looked very distressed while she was telling me all that, right then a thought surged in my mind, in addition to many others, I tried to give her a little encouragement, support and understanding to get her out of the state she was in, for reasons beyond her control, I told her not to worry that she would have a better and bigger home.

"The most important thing is that nothing happened to you and your family, the most precious treasure of a person is their life and that of their loved ones, and you still have that." She told me, "all that was left were ashes, and there was nothing but ashes."

I understand, but wherever there are ashes build a ladder to climb wherever you want, remember that you only lost material things, you and your family are alive, while you are alive you can get all that was lost and much more. My interest was to release the lady of her anguish and despair, in my mind I knew that her situation was very difficult, she was desperate, tears flooded her eyes, sadness and pain took hold of her. She was submerged in so much pain that she did not seem to realize that she was still alive and that nothing had happened to her family, thank God the words of encouragement I told her made her react, she finally stopped crying and her eyes took on a luster similar to the brightness of the sun in spring. The words that God put in me to give to her, succeeded in making her come back to reality. Sometimes when things happen to people something as serious as what happened to her, anguish overwhelms them to such degree that they forget that they are still alive and that nothing will be, nor is more valuable than life. The strikes in the lives of people, does not give them the time to pause and think that they must continue, that material things are necessary, but nothing compares to life itself, because when one can enjoy the privilege so great that God has given us, the other things become tiny and fleeting, that everything can be achieved again, there is a great challenge, you must continue despite the circumstances and adverse situations, you must draw strength from where there is none left. I just want to remind you, that you have the opportunity to read this line, that while you have life you can get everything, whether you have lost it or have never had it; all the treasures and valuable things in the world belong to every human being without distinction. Do not let the despair and pain take away the opportunity to look ahead. And to think that all is not lost, the lady even forgot that the insurance would give him another home, she could not think straight, but even then in the middle of the disaster there is still hope, even if your belongings are not ensured, as long as there's life there will always be plenty of time to get everything you want in life.

Starting from nothing will never be easy, but a human value that is solidarity has not yet been lost, there are always people willing to cooperate and extend their help in one way or another, not everything is lost, the most important of a human being is life, there will always be time to start over. Do not let discouragement; depression and sadness take over you. Make of your ashes a ladder, I assure you that with positive thinking and a tenacious mind you will be able to climb to the last rung of that ladder and beyond.

You possess invincible weapons

Both the people and the inner animals have weapons, in the case of the predatory animals of the forest, they put in place a series of actions to catch their prey. Where they are really amazing, lions and cheetahs; they really have an uncanny ability when catching their prey. In the case of people, they have many more tools and weapons and most invincible, just imagine how powerful of a weapon your mind is, the one is so strong, no one can enter it to scrutinize what you are thinking, for the time being at least because in the future there will be some machine or instrument that can decipher what people are thinking, just know that for now that weapon is yours, it is powerful and almost indestructible, so please, because it is so powerful use it to do good, your mind is a weapon much more powerful than those sold in stores, and the one you have no one can snatch, your mind is impenetrable. Who can invade your thoughts? I do not think there is a weapon more powerful than the one you have, your mind.

And what do say of this, that most people do not even realize they have it, that inner strength that we all carry inside, regardless of race, color or whoever the person is. Another weapon is wisdom, which every human being has, without exception, it's a wisdom and intelligence of their own, and that no one can take away. To smile, listen and remain silent at any given moment, becomes other types of invincible and powerful weapons, when one remains silent before aggressive and loud people. One demonstrates to have great power, and when one does not respond to personal aggression from others, one has won the battle, without having to resort to violent means.

By smiling in the midst of adversity, is a weapon that heals the deepest wounds and destroys anxiety, stress and despair. Listening, not everyone has the gift of listening, everyone wants to be heard, to speak, speak and speak, everyone speaks, and very few people know how to listen.

If parents listened to their young children and adolescents, they would avoid themselves many headaches, bad times, sleepless nights and suffering. Knowing how to listen, besides becoming a weapon of great power is a divine privilege, a gift given by God, why a weapon of great power? because by stopping to listen to someone allows you to know the problem that is happening, giving you the tools and guidelines to help solve their problems and you could even have the opportunity to save a life and who knows possibly more; even if you are not a counselor or behavioral professional. When someone tries to assault you with their dimes and directives, hurtful words and personal offenses, do not surrender to their games, use your powerful and indestructible weapons, why waste time arguing with someone who's only intention is to hurt you, and offend who they can, not who they want to, use your invincible and invisible darts that magnify whoever has them. Have you ever known a weapon more powerful than tolerance, patience, mental strength, positivism, altruism, loyalty and honesty? If you resort to those weapons that you cannot buy in stores, there will surely be no opponent that can beat you. And what is best it is that when you make use of your invincible weapons it will help prevent future problems, you will not have to be involved in difficulties, in having to apologize or give excuses, although it is not too much to ask for an apology when someone has been offended or has offended. Do not put victory on a silver platter for your opponent, responding with aggression, if you use your invisible weapons, if you know how to use them at the right moment, you are assured victory. These are weapons of a high caliber and invincible. There's your life raft

Run in search of your dreams

Worldwide, there is a lot of competition on the planet from competitors competing for first place, most of them training nights and days to obtain a medal at the Olympic Games, a gold or silver medal. Others are in competition for reasons unknown to the audience, but the person who is running has a reason that is solely their own, exclusive to that person, has their own interest and motivation independently of that of the others, each one of those people who know why they are doing it, it is not easy for them to train, much less compete when it comes down to running, however, almost all people who run after a dream, have achieved great things and have overcome risky obstacles, managing to see all their dreams come true.

You, like all those runners, are not the exception, get up, run in search of your dreams, get cheer up, put all your efforts in, go after your dreams, do not stop, run with all your might, your commitment, your enthusiasm, invest all of your energy as the great runners do, when they want to win the competition, even if you do not have other competitors, but I assure you that there will always be competitors, even if you do not believe it, many people are fighting and want to become and have that you want most, and they must not be judged, we live in a competitive and changing world that spins at a high speed, in a competitive society everyone has the same right to want to advance, because every day new opportunities appear and only those who have prepared can opt for them.

The fact that others want the same thing as you is no reason to stop running after your dreams, but be steady in achieving what your dreams really are not what others want, if you do not keep fighting for yours, at the end of that race you will want to look for a new track to run the race of your dreams. Fight, work, for your dreams with a little self-confidence and a good attitude, you will be able to cross the boundaries, overcome all obstacles and when you have finished running after your dreams you will feel the satisfaction, well-being and happiness of having succeeded. Follow, do not look back even if your opponent is yourself, many times people do not achieve what they want because they live in a constant struggle with themselves, nothing really to do with anyone else.

Run after your dreams, if you are the obstacle you find on the running track defeat yourself, run faster than usual, time could become a potential enemy, competing with yourself is the biggest challenge a person can have, you will be forced to develop sufficient skills, abilities and be willing not to lose the competition, at the end you will be qualified, experienced, the rest will be simpler, because you will have defeated the main enemy that opposed you, yourself.

The big competitions are done on the running track; anywhere else would be a waste of time. Life itself is a challenge, every day we must fight to be alive and have good quality of life, daily living with its pro and cons is one, the track where the runners must fight to reach the finish line, all of us on this planet earth must run with iron decision to be able to overcome all the obstacles that appear on the track of life to reach our dreams.

You, who has not yet taken the initiative; get up, get to your feet, believe in yourself, in who you are, in your potential; set the strategies, choices and energy that you have in motion, to achieve the realization of this project that runs through your mind. Run in search of your dreams.

A positive and optimistic attitude clears up the way on a stony ground

A positive attitude and disposition, and a life full of optimism, are of paramount importance in reaching a goal, an enthusiastic and happy person despite the circumstances that are seizing their life, already has 50% of the triumph guaranteed and in their hands. You only have to start working, with the security, the confidence and the certainty that in a short or long term your wishes will come true. Sowing in your mind a small little seed bathed in positivism and enthusiasm, putting in place an arduous plan of work, accompanied by good preparation, responsibility, perseverance and courage, will already have most of the journey traveled, even if the journey path was stony. Every person individually has the potential and the ability to succeed in the trait or area of interest. To believe that you can, the power is in you, not to faint before the obstacles, as it is a part of the lives of some people more than others. Without those obstacles no one would know how strong they are and how many things they are capable of doing, obstacles are like stones in the rivers, we have never seen a river without stones in it. They along with the water make up the river, that is how inconveniences work, they are part of the lives of most people, without them one would not know how much has been achieved and what challenges one has been encountered with; or how far preparation the key for success has come, there is nothing more powerful to break down barriers than to prepare by studying, age does not matter, nor race, color or anything similar, study knocks down more walls than the great machines or the more sophisticated instruments. A vast academic education accompanied with a good family up bringing will become a stronger tool than a tractor with its great sharp blades; they are capable of making spaces, removing debris, stones and weeds from the road. If you prepare yourself you will be able to open the doors even if they have a lock. Dreams can be achieved; parameters and size will depend on what each person wants individually. While not forgetting that we are social entities and without the help, cooperation and presence of society in general, it would not be impossible, but your growth would not have the magnitude then if you have the support of the community. A positive and optimistic attitude clears up the way on a stony ground.

Sow in fertile ground

When we use altruism and take the causes of others as if they were ours, we are contributing to others developing, to fulfill their desires and achieve their goals.

Helping others in the way they need it most, at any time in your lives regardless of whether they are family, known to you or not, cooperating with other people is a good way to sow in fertile ground, without expecting that that someone you have helped will return the fruits of your labor. It is not an investment where you put in a certain amount of time or money to then rip the gains. It is not a type of business, be supportive and cooperate with the problems of others.

It is something where, even if you do not believe it, could take you as far as you propose, because even if you do not receive a reward from those people whom you have helped, understanding, solidarity, believe it or not, everything will be returned to you by divine order, the universe is immense, but it has the characteristic that it gives back everything that you have done in favor of the causes of those people who at a moment in their lives have needed it. In case you do not receive the greatness and gratitude from the universe, there always is the case of your future generations, it is for that reason that we must act the best we can, because they inherit everything, the favorable and the unfavorable, is the law of the universe. Everything we give to others will come back a good deal and multiplied by 100%.

I am sure that all my generations to come will be blessed and prosperous, not because I have done much good, but because I try not to hurt anyone, I know that they will always have food because I have taken over the task since I was very young to feed the birds and any other animal I would find hungry. I have my own birds I feed, oh, do not misunderstand me, in the same way I love freedom in a personal way, they also want and prefer their freedom, no one likes captivity, so if you have some caged birds offer them a better world, give them their freedom, that is a very good action. You can keep your own birds, because when you give them food they themselves come back to you, there is no need to trap them, wherever I have lived I have fed the birds, the wild ones, they come to me, because I always put food and some water out for them. They already discriminate the fact that they can go look for food somewhere else, but they do not waste food because I give them what they need, it gives me great pleasure to see them happy and they make me happy, but they come and leave, they are free like the air, like the wind.

In my country I went to the parks to feed the pigeons, in Santo Domingo many parks are full of pigeons, because people go there to pass the time and to feed them. I'm not telling you to do this, no, everyone is different and for this reason we all do different things, but for me in particular is something that gives me much happiness, to see them eat, in my city I never wasted rice or bread, as I had a nice patio I always put that out for the birds and they not only came to eat, but some made nests in an orange tree that was in the house, it could be something insignificant, but if it fed the birds, it helped them reproduce and also contributed to them keeping the environment clean. Knowing that no bird will die for lack of food is something divine. God is the one who feeds the birds; the fact that they come to where I am gives me great joy. To hear them sing, fighting with each other for the space, or the food, some do not want to let the others eat, others seem to have young ones because they only take a small portion and leave. It would be good to not only do this with the birds, if it is within our reach why not share our food with other people, many children and adults lack food, they suffer hunger in this world, others die for lack of food, and if we as human beings only passing through this land, and have the joy and the opportunity to help someone, with at least being able to help one person, we will be able to offer them a better quality of life, he who receives a greater reward, is the one who has stripped themselves of something to share it with that person who although today is missing something material is as valuable as you who has everything.

Sowing in fertile soil is not only done on the ground when trees and ornamental and edible fruits are planted, one can sow by helping people, when it is not possible to do so with one thing there will always be another way to be able to cooperate with, just by being a good example in life one is already sowing for those future generations to follow your good example, cultivating human values is also a very good way to sow. Do not look at nation, race, religion, sex, color or sexual orientation, or any other condition. As the rain falls over all plants the same, never classifying them, it allows them to grow and stay green and beautiful, and as the sun too it shines for everyone in a general sense. The stars and the moon illuminate the whole universe equally. We human beings who have the capacity to think and reason, let's not make exceptions towards people when it comes to helping them, let's be supportive, cooperative and altruistic with who needs it the most and at the precise time that is required. Always sow in fertile ground. Do not give up on doing well by others; it is a very beautiful dream.

Yes, it's possible, never stop dreaming

The word "impossible" remove it from your internal dictionary that is, from your soul, your mind, instead replace with: "yes, you can". There are no limits to those who dream. When you have dreams it is imperative to shed your disbelief, it will not lead you anywhere when you doubt what you are capable of doing, to believe that you can do it will be the first step to be able to ascend to that preponderant place where you want to go. Effort and constant work serve as a push to get you on your way to the finish line.

Do nothing, stand still, think negatively, leads to failure and defeat, no matter how simple your yearning, give your thinking a change, never stop dreaming, if you have dreamed of the peace and tranquility of your life, of your family and everything around you, do not think it's impossible. If there is someone who thinks that nobody ever dreams of having peace and that it is a very simple feat, only possesses a closed minded way of thinking, because millions and millions of people in the world flee from their places of birth and the only thing they pursue is a little peace. Because peace is necessary to live a quiet, even life, a heart that dwells in the middle of stillness, favors people because they have their lives secured for a longer time, meanwhile where there is no peace, no quietness, a person subjected to stress, anxiety and constant despair have a lesser chance of life.

Many people in the world desire the peace within their homes, their personal life and that of their countries. Having the peace and tranquility that human beings deserve could become the dream of many. If you believe that everything

61

is possible, if you dedicate your time to it, effort accompanied by work, because he who dreams and does nothing to achieve it, will get nothing in return, like in the case of someone who wants to lose weight, they should not place their focus on how much they weigh, they should do what is necessary to lose weight. In all the things you want to be or have, certain rules apply, let's imagine that a person wants to be a lawyer, for that they must register in a university that offers that career and apply all the rules and conditions that it requires of in this case; or if you want to be a catwalk model, just wanting it is not going to help achieve it, you will have to work to detail the skills needed to be a catwalk model, in short, all dreams require effort, dedication, constancy, motivation and love. Because without putting in love for what you want it will be very difficult to achieve that goal, you will be stranded halfway, fatigue, reluctance and apathy will overcome you. Another factor to take into account is that most professions require an initial investment of money, but when you invest in education, whether it is for your children or for yourself, although it might be for the long run it is the best investment that anyone can make.

The money that is invested in education is like a seed, although that seed might take a while for being so small and it takes its time to grow, in due time it will bear fruit. The academic preparation opens the doors, in case they are closed at that time being for whatever reason or circumstance, surely days later other opportunities will open up. Studies should be a priority to which attention must be paid; it is one of the greatest planting processes that a person can do while they are alive. No one can take from you or your children what is learned, it is something that belongs to each individual, but if you cannot study do not worry, there are many other dreams that you can achieve. If you have not achieved your dreams as a young person do not give up, there is always time, believe that you can, take the word "impossible" out of your mind, the correct word is "I can", perhaps you may not be able to hurry, at the speed of the wind, because each person's circumstances are different, if you cannot run, then walk, it will probably take a little longer, but just the same you will reach the finish line.

Observe the turtles, they never run and or walk fast, the point is that where ever they decide to go, they get there, and they have the faculty that since they go slowly, they get a glimpse of where the dangers on the road are, so they are protected and last for years, many more years. They take their time they do not succumb to despair, they are persevering, what I am trying to capture here is, that if it is not feasible to achieve a certain dream in the real world, there is much more, everything is possible, most of the things that are wanted take time, and even if you have large amounts of money you have to wait. As when a seed is planted, when a baby is born, it must be well cared for and needs time to grow, no one becomes an adult if they were not a child before, and that requires of some time and space. Parents' money will provide amenities, care and good diet, but it will not help it grow. Dreams are the same way, you have to wait, if you do not wait you will not see what you want, everything you want needs time, but it does not mean that you can leave it and then go back to it later, it is not what they are. All people have the same opportunity and the same rights, but those rights bring with them duties, investment, dedication, work and efforts. Yes you can, never stop dreaming.

Create your own opportunity

If you are walking the path of life and you have not yet gotten a chance to create your dream, or develop your talent, I want you to know that all the people that inhabit the planet earth without taking into account their age, color, sex or sexual preference, one thing has no relation to the other, far from who you are, or can be, whether or not you have purchasing power, all people have their own talent, that something so special that no one can take away, because it belongs to each one of us individually, an inalienable right that no other being can take away. In the same measure that you are important, is also in the same way you can develop and do something of great importance for yourself. It could even be to the benefit of the community and humanity. If your talent has nothing to do with that that already exists, much better, you are an innovator, think, do not get stuck as a ship adrift without doing something, you will not be on planet earth without doing something, stand up straight and act decisively.

Leave aside any setbacks that occur, start developing that talent you have. Undoubtedly it is valuable, we all have one, look to see what yours is to begin working on that project, do not think that you do not own one, all humans came each with their own. Even the flowers do, have you observed that all are different and each of them have different odors, they have different functions, some serve to make perfumes, others adorn gardens in houses. The wild ones adorn the fields and prairies, oils are extracted of others and a series of more things that they realize as they came with their own functions. And what to say about the organs of the body, both inside and outside, they each perform a different task, each one has its own activity, neither has to envy anything from the others. The feet can rarely do the same as the hands and vice versa, and the kidneys do not do the function of the liver, the heart cannot do the work that is solely owned by the brain and so on, all our organs inside and outside the body exert a very important role in each person, if we lacked any of them there would be an imbalance and we could even get sick.

Stand up if you're sitting, I apologize for daring to tell you, it's that I want to have a good relationship with you right now, a little trust, get up from where you're sitting, begin to dream, anything, there are so many as there are fish at the bottom of the sea, all it takes is a little bit of an idea, initiative, determination, spontaneity. Let's go back to the activities, the eyes cannot hear; they can only observe, they can only see, the ears cannot do what the eyes do. In the same way that people came with their own talent, at first, their idea could be like a tiny mustard seed, but in the end it has every chance to become bigger than a house, although a person may have different skills and talents, many different roles can be performed, but it would not be advisable to remain without doing anything, while complaining, shouting and being fitful one cannot go forward, many people get lost in life through lamenting and doing nothing for themselves or for others. So many things of life are important and necessary and that can be done in benefit of it and of others. If you cannot do something with your hands, you can always give someone the gift of a "good morning", a smile, making someone smile is already something very beautiful, many people in the world are so sad and overwhelmed that they have forgotten to smile, if you have the talent to cheer someone up, that is of great value, but there are still so many other things and activities that you can do, do not stay stuck there where you are, think, what can I do for myself and for others.

All human beings have the capacity to perform in multiple trades and it is true that in the world many have done the same tasks it is just that each one is unique, and as such a thinking and creative person one will have their own peculiar way of doing what they do, without the need to imitate others, everyone can do the same work, but each one possess a different way of doing what they do, there are many lawyers, doctors, engineers, presidents, masons, painters, writers, laborers. They who always get my attention, because what would be of the world without these groups of artists who farm the lands? without anyone taking them into account, worldwide on a daily basis they give everything of themselves, they enter the fertile fields for cultivation with dedication and great care to till and sow seeds with an infinite love, because we do not all possess that fine talent to sow the land, that it is something so beautiful and important for all humanity.

Ah! But I could not do what they do, that is a talent that only special people possess. How would we do it if no one possessed such a great capacity to love people so much as to dedicate themselves to furrowing and planting so that people all over the earth could feed themselves? If people did not eat, they could get sick, die, hopefully someday we'll think about all those artists that help us to be healthy, from our food depends on how much we can live and how healthy we can be. Being a day laborer is a great talent, which we do not all have, but that we must thank those artists who do not sleep or eat well, just thinking how to grow vegetables and everything else people put on their tables every day, without thinking about those delicate hands that are now stripped of their softness, they made the grooves, sowed the seeds, watered them, sleepless wondering if they would sprout, if they would grow healthy, the day laborers themselves cultivated, cared for and reaped the fruits of the land. I want you as you work the land to not feel any less able, that those who perform another function in the world, all the trades that are performed with love, effort, dignity, are important and the people who perform them as well. No talent is less than another; you have the opportunity to create yours.

Nothing is too small that it cannot have value, nor so great as to not be able to acquire value, to move others, look how small the ants are, they are on this planet with their own function, we may not give them the importance they have and require, but for reason unknown to me, they are here, alongside humans. If you do not have the talent to grow flowers, vegetables, stems, you can do other things that will be needed, if not now in the future, or you can start a business, do not worry if at the beginning it is small, it will grow as the trees grow, as bamboo grows, at first it is stagnant under the earth, as if it were never going to grow out of there, but then it takes on a huge height, incredible to believe, study, take care of, little animals not all can do something like this, take care of children, the elderly people, that talent of caring for our most valuable treasures, the elderly people, not everyone has that gift, what would it be of the many people who cannot clean their houses, but find someone who does such valuable work, for that, great love and a great talent is necessary, the cleaning of homes, public and private spaces is a necessity, many people throughout the universe have this valuable function for leaving things that shine as if they were new again. I do not want to tell you to go do what you do not want to do, but if you perform that function do not feel less than others who do other things, you and your work are important, not all of us can do it. Imagine that there were not those valuable and important people who perform the role in the world of collecting our waste, yes those we put out on the curb on the streets on the day to be picked up, if there were no people willing to do this work, all humanity in general would get sick, with the same waste that we all discard and that we call garbage.

They, the dedicated people, although someone might not agree, contribute for the cities to stay clean, free of epidemics and diseases. Does it not seem to you that that's a great talent? To me it is, not all human beings could perform such commendable work. If you still do not know what your task is, if you have not yet created a way of life, in no way would I ever tell someone to dream of collecting our waste, what I am saying is that it is a worthy job like any other and that those who do it deserve our recognition, consideration and respect.

You are just in time, no matter what age you are or on what part of the planet you are, whatever your race, color, nationality, sex, origin, if you can read, you could be a great genius and you have not discovered it yet.

Intelligence comes with humans and even animals possess an exceptional intelligence, of course that the intelligence of people surpasses that of other living beings.

A new way of thinking, a vision, can change your life and that of others, with your ingenuity you could achieve an invention that in the future could change and save the lives of other people or humanity as a whole. Many people, perhaps millions, who never imagined having great endowments, supernatural intelligence, something out of the ordinary in childhood, never imagining they would become scientists.

Some great inventors, through the time of the years and centuries, still live today, because they have left their legacies in medicine, technology, as in various areas of building knowledge. And that whole range of abundance in different facts, today we all enjoy those thousands of things that others have left for the world. Do not believe that you cannot do it, you always can, you and no one else can create that chance to succeed and be successful in what you undertake. Thinking that something as big as what someone else has done is not for you, turn the coin to heads, you will see that it says yes you can, and the opportunities are for everyone, the only drawback is that not everyone is willing to work with determination, commitment, responsibility and dedication. If you want to start a company save a little money, start with something small, if at this time you do not have enough money to make a big corporation, however small it starts, one day it will grow. Look at the babies at birth, they are tiny, with love and care as time goes by they develop; they grow and grow so big that the mother is surprised, how much that baby has grown. Get enthused, be sure to not get stuck there doing nothing, do something fruitful, if you cannot study for the moment or start a company, there are many things that at first seem very difficult, but practice makes it easy. In case the possibility of success has not knocked at your door at this time, go out in search of it, seek help, there are plenty of people willing to give their helping hand in return of nothing, in the world there are many disadvantages, the good thing is that not everything is damaged yet. There are always people who selflessly cooperate and lend their help to others without asking for anything in return.

Throughout the world, many people donate their money so that others have the opportunity to study and prepare. Sometimes opportunity knocks at the doors of some people, gets tired of knocking, withdraws because no one opens it, other times it does not knock, simply passes, because it only stops where it can find its friend education, in that particular field and that the person is willing to strive, studying or working, or like those who win the lottery, before anything they must buy a ticket. You have to invest at least your energy. Create your own opportunity.

Build your empire

You cannot build a building overnight; all construction takes prudent time, even if you have all the tools, materials and a huge number of people to do the building. Nothing appears by magic, to build an empire is a process, it is like building a great building, you cannot do it in a day because in all the constructions certain rules apply, so that it does not collapse with a natural phenomenon, or because the necessary measures where not taken, to avoid building defects, with the permission of experts in this area, if you want to form your own empire you must invest time, dedication, efforts and perhaps a little money, but most of all, bravery, losing the fear to start and perhaps that of failure, it may be that at the beginning things do not go as expected. Fear is harmful even when just in need of crossing the streets, if you have to cross a street in the city and think that you can get run over, those negative thoughts can ensure that something bad does happens to you, but when crossing a road it should not be done in the middle of the road, that is what the zebra lines or white stripes are for but you must wait for the pedestrian signal to walk and especially wait for the traffic light to turn red.

Fear is a mortal enemy that can spoil and kill even the greatest desires of success. By destroying people's confidence in the potential they have, it could end with their self-esteem. No one is exempt from realizing and creating something, he who did not come with aptitudes for one thing has them for another, in diversity and differences is where the beauty of life itself lies, the world would not be a world if all people were dedicate to do the same thing. What would happen to the others? Surely there would be chaos. People have millions of possibilities to make and achieve a place in the world, if they dare, lose the fear of falls and stumbles, falls and great walls are likely to occur, just as there are millions of ways to get up and seek strategies to cross the great walls.

When I was working in a middle school in my country of birth I was giving a talk to a group of 40 teenagers, within that talk I asked some questions, including: what would they do if they were trapped by a very high wall whose walls seemed invincible and impossible to climb and within its walls a fierce lion with the sole intention of catching and devouring them? Some responded immediately, I would let it catch me as there is nothing else left to do, others said I would kill the lion, a few said, oh, I would tame the lion! Others said, I either kill the lion or look up a way to climb the wall. My only intention was to know how each of them would react when faced with a difficulty. Those who responded that they would allow to just be caught, belonged to the group of people who stop in the face of difficult and compromising situations, without seeing that there will always be an option, while the response of the others made it clear that they could solve their own problems in one way or another, without letting themselves be defeated, rather their positive ways led them to seek alternatives so as not to let themselves be ruined.

You would say why do I bring this up? When one suggests building an empire, always, if one does not have the sufficient strength and the necessary evenness when the drawbacks come, that in every day of people's lives there will always be one way or another, it will take you much more time to build your empire. However, if you change the discourse in your mind by bathing it with decision, courage, a deep touch of enthusiasm and positivism, laying solid foundations to build your empire, making sure that nothing and no one destroys what you have achieved with your own efforts, avoiding the naysayers that always come up to you telling you that this or that thing will not produce profit, or money, that that thing you want there is already enough of that in the community, in the city, in the surroundings, when the disheartening people come to rob you of your energy, your dreams, do not pay attention, go ahead with your project.

With the construction of your empire, do not let anyone stop you, place that first stone, if you do not have it in your hands look for it somewhere on the planet, do not be inert, thinking that you cannot do it, that the conditions are not right, for each person there are one and thousands of possibilities, discover yours. Transform your mind, if you still do not feel sure, just know that you can, do not leave it to time, time is more valuable than gold, you can buy gold, but you can never buy time. Start now; strength, enthusiasm, courage, has the power and ability to destroy the walls and the highest and most difficult barriers that may exist. Build your empire.

Victory belongs to those who fight hard

Thousands and millions of people around the world since their young age feel within themselves an arduous desire to reach an ideal, a force that drives them to fight for things that perhaps for others seem unattainable, anyone would think that children do not have dreams, that the desire for success is only allowed to adults, those great goals that at first sight seem impossible. The fact is that most of the population of children have dreams, sometimes it is they who have dreams and ideals that surpasses the nature and the human mind, when a child has dreams you and all of us could ensure that that little human dreamer, is already a winner and sooner rather than later can achieve all that he or she wants, it is that the little worm that is inside you, telling you that you can, that you are able to achieve the highest and greatest feats, to be a child is not an impediment to dreaming, the dreams of the little ones at their young age are as great as those of the adults, although some have to wait to grow, surely they will wait, they will continue with their dreams and when the propitious time arrives they will reach it. Adults are more likely to stop fighting.

Some people give up easier when what they want becomes difficult, or things get complicated. On the other hand children are not afraid to wait, they are brave, overcomers, if they do not understand something they are not afraid to ask, they observe the adults when they too are learning, they try to do them as well or better than some adults, because children do what they have to do; compassion, enthusiasm, with a few exceptions, but we have known of children who have gone beyond the limits reached, achievements out of this world and I do not mean those who are gifted, those who have an IQ above others, those young children with special skills. Many of the children who do not fit in the normal classroom simply came with an outstanding ability and sometimes we do not understand them, and labeled them as abnormal. Genius children, but I make reference to those who have the intelligence of the majority, children who often live in broken homes, others in hostile homes and some that the economic possibilities of their parents are not adequate for children to succeed, other children who although the purchasing power exists in their homes, do not receive the affection and care and attention that children need to be healthy and useful adults in society; nevertheless they overcome, they have dreams, they pursue them and their courage, constancy takes them to the top of the summit. They, who put eagerness, ardor, firmness and passion into their work, their studies, even when the conditions are not the best for one reason or another,

Those who dare to take advantage of all the difficulties of life, those that are driven by the strength of achieving, the craving and desire to get ahead. Children who want to be good people when they grow up, they have goals, dreams, many of them that are adults today have defied all disasters and setbacks in the way, and others that are still young today, but that think of achievements much larger than their own size due to their young age. There are these kinds of children all over the planet, they are not specific to any country, nation, city, community, region, town, neighborhood or corner of the world, and they are everywhere. Of them there are many in the whole world, exceptional worthy of all admiration. We adults should never stop dreaming, when you are an adult you have the ability, the tenacity, and the ability to fight strong and hard, to fight and make victory yours. In daily life each person individually has a melee, where the constant game that is lived does not stop, attacks relentlessly, adults who present different situations in the course of their life that seems to have no solution, believe me in that as distant as one might seem there will always be an exit, even if they are not measured with the naked eye, the exit will always be there waiting for you to start the journey, but keep in mind where you want to go.

Never go without a fixed course, draw goals, objectives, no one buys a travel ticket without knowing where they are going, keep your banner up; a starting point must be accompanied by another arrival. The choices of a person wherever they are in the world, that driving force, that resolution of continuous struggle is what will allow them to obtain the victory in a world where it is very true that it is full of opportunities, the competition is of giant size and to overcome a giant it is not so easy. Stay steadfast in your desires of continuous struggle, to be able to sustain yourself in battle. Do not get tired or faint, do not let yourself be taken by discouragement, think like children, they do not know tiredness or exhaustion when they are chasing something, they are not discouraged even when they are told by adults that they cannot do something, children are insistent, constant, they do not resist, they do not know fear; fight, without battle there is no victory and victory belongs to those who fight hard.

Get ready to reach the top and achieve success

There is no established recipe for success, because it is the result of good preparation, hard work, continuous work, constancy, a titanic work, the sum of falling, and getting back up, overcoming difficulties and obstacles. All the people who then and now have been successful in different areas have had to deal with powerful monsters that have crossed their path at some point in their lives. I speak of the ghost of failure, one way or another, but they did not plunge into depression. They did not waste their time regretting; they knew how to raise their forehead with great dexterity, courage and enthusiasm. When they have stumbled and fallen, without a moment's hesitation, they have risen to their feet in a hopeful spirit, full of faith; without falling into recrimination, knowing that in order to climb a hill, the more elevated, will have more difficulties; but in the end, if they do not stop, they will be able to feel and savor the happiness of having achieved it. Success goes and meets those who launch themselves and work to achieve it. Success without effort is not success, because nothing has been invested.

For a beautiful garden to bloom and give beautiful flowers it must be taken care of, it is necessary that one devotes time to it, if not, in a short amount of time all the flowers will wither and the garden will disappear.

To reach a dream it requires of work and time of dedication, to have the certainty that you will get it, believing that you already have in your hands that which you have longed for; and not neglect it once achieved, so that it remains just as alive as its first day.

The universe has created millions and billions of opportunities tailored to each person. Everything is there waiting for those who wish to achieve success. The triumph does not belong to a particular group, no, the opportunities are limitless, there are there for everyone, and different ones.

Think, analyze, scrutinize, and go out looking for the one that belongs to you. There is one that is especially yours; do not forget that it requires a minimum of effort on your part, preparation, and investment. Whether we want it or not, we must pay a price for what we want, nothing falls from the clouds. Whatever your area of interest, you will have to do something for your own cause. Some dreams only require time, others a high dose of imagination and ideas, but everything needs perseverance, responsibility, commitment and that that should never be lacking: effective work. Achieving success does not necessarily mean obtaining money, a large company or material things; all that could be the sum of a myriad of achievements. Succeeding goes further than that, it is something greater than material possessions.

Acquiring wisdom is an achievement and a dream that many people in the world value.

Knowing is a power that transcends limits and opens spaces, even if they are tightly closed. Knowing goes beyond simple knowledge, but success is different for each person in a particular way; for some it could be summed up to have a full and happy life, to be satisfied with how little or how much has been achieved. Success is more a part of being, than of having; even though some people are more concerned about having, than being. To have is a state of mind; today you can have everything that any human being could wish for in order to feel fulfilled and satisfied. It is not bad to worry about material goods, because no one can live without money and the things that can be bought with it, but there must be a balance between both, we cannot forget to cultivate our being. Being and having are very different things, and each one keeps a great distance with the other. You can lose what you have in an instant, for different reasons, even when you are not prepared for the mountain to come crumbling down, all that for what you have fought and worked for. Being is very different; when you are it, it is forever. Many hearts go around the world full of joy, enthusiasm, happiness, solidarity, and with a series of values that there is no fire, earthquake, or storm that can destroy it, because it is something within, intrinsic within your interior, within your character, your personality. To achieve success through the being, full of joy, and satisfaction; hopefully we can all work to obtain and have everything we dream of, to do it with tenacity, keen awareness and enthusiasm, without forgetting the being. Being a better human being is priceless, not bought or sold.

The only obstacle between you and your dreams, is you

We have already talked about the obstacles that prevent someone from crossing from one place to another.

After a natural phenomenon, depending on the magnitude and its category, everything left in the middle of the tracks, roads, streets and ways, all the debris left in its way, fallen trees and all debris obstruct the tracks and holts the traffic.

As much of the people, as of the vehicles, as great and strong as the machineries can be, same thing happens in the lives of some people, independently of the conditions that they have had to live; some bad ones, some good ones, and others terribly worse, that paralyze the person and prevents them from advancing and growing in any activity they try to carry out.

However, in most cases, when it is about achieving a dream, the only obstacle in achieving a goal, is the person themselves, for various reasons, sometimes economic resources serve as a barrier to the person, even if they really want it, they will not get to have that that they desire.

Of course there are variables that people cannot control. Many situations are unexpected, such as family losses and illness, and countless problems that must be faced, which are likely to turn the whole environment upside down, and which cannot be controlled at that certain moment, but there are others that can be controlled, and are totally dependent on the person themselves; and the lack of interest which has nothing to do with traumatic events, but rather for lack of faith, hope; for fear of what others will say if things do not turn out as expected. Thoughts are a nuisance that hinders passage, even if the roads are wide open, and all forecasts point to all the options and the possibilities of reaching a certain goal. A change of attitude in your thoughts, dismissing the doubts are of paramount importance so that you yourself do not become the impediment that does not allow yourself to obtain a specific good, academic or any category. Every person who puts in their part, works hard in order to have something, has all the right and the power to achieve it.

The "what if's" are part of life itself; there are no obstacles, mountains, or walls that no human being cannot overcome. Do not look at problems and setbacks with contempt and disdain; look at it as something favorable, without their presence one would not know that one is a winner, or that you are someone who does not fear challenges. How would you know that you have climbed to the top if you have never been to the outskirts of the hill? Difficulties, even if you do not believe it, have their own benefits; each of them already brings their teaching moment, some lesson we need to learn before climbing to the highest peak. If it disturbs you, you cannot take advantage of it, what do they bring with them; the turbulence makes the person stronger, say no to discouragement and apathy. The only obstacle between you and your dreams is you.

Make way in the middle of the rubble

Most adults have had the unpleasant opportunity to see, even if just through the media, the disasters, the debris, garbage and all kinds of waste that a hurricane or a storm leave after passing through a city or country. Some have been so large and devastating that they have left behind unfortunate losses and a gloomy, bleak and painful panorama. Sometimes it has been so strong that it has taken months and years, in some extreme situations, to achieve the total recovery of the city and especially of the people. However, even if all this disaster of nature has passed, people have the obligation to continue the daily process of their lives, and have to open a gap to be able to move from one place to another, because despite all the devastation, the train of life should not stop.

Millions of people around the world have an ardent desire to go in search of a dream, with a strong will to move, to cross from one place to another, to give their own a better quality of life.

People who have broken all schemes; defying adversity, whose willpower transcends the limits of human understanding. We have seen people succeed despite lacking a part of their body, or of one of their senses. And people who since their childhood have had to fight alone, without the help or support of a relative, but have become great heroes. I call them that, because he who overcomes the mishaps that their existence has brought to them, whose audacity has allowed them to defy the setbacks and abrupt moments they have faced throughout their short or long life. It is very true that the world in which we live in has often been intricate and complex for some people, more than for others, but that is no cause or reason for not dreaming. Having dreams will even serve to lengthen your existence on the planet, because when someone is motivated, they are much more likely to live longer; it's that even when you are ill, a good disposition and a great dose of positivism end with even the most complicated diseases.

And what to say if reaching achievement is what it is about. If a person, whoever they may be, thinks that what they want to have or achieve will come true, they have already won the first part, the first step is already in place; the rest will be to work and do what is necessary to make it concrete.

Almost all people, when they try to cross certain streets and avenues, have the possibility of finding them clear of obstacles. But we must not forget that these are streets where we all have the same right; this supposes that you can find congestion and traffic, but not for that reason will you stop. Although waiting might have to happen, you will have to continue to be able to leave from there successful and triumphant from that place. Difficulties and impediments wherever people find themselves are in the light of day; tumbles and rubble are likely on the road to wherever we try to advance to. Many are those who stop at the first hurdles; however they are many more that have defied all adversity. From the inaccessible routes they have proposed to rise with the crown or the medal for which they have exerted themselves. No one has ever been told that things will be easy and or that one will get what is wanted, or that it will fall like rain. And notice that it rains when it is cloudy. It means that for something to happen, another action is required before hand. However, perseverance, work, previous preparation, motivation and a positive mind, with an eagerness for triumph, these are able to remove the trunks and debris from the roads, which have been left behind by a phenomenon of nature or a life's moment as deplorable as it may be.

You are a strong, valuable, important human being; try to overcome, rise yourself through any impediment, it is not easy to rise from an unfavorable situation, but it is possible when it is fought with determination and keen awareness.

Make way in the middle of the rubble.

Believe in your dreams

If there is something so powerful to make any dream that you dream come true, it is to believe, place in your mind that idea, that worm that makes the wheels roll around in your head, indicating that what you want is a fact. Begin to thank God for that that you dream to achieve. Being grateful to the creator makes him to command the universe to set in motion, working in his favor.

So that you may have the reward dreamed of, believe that it is already there in your hands; Even if it seems distant, even if you do not have the minimum conditions to achieve it and all the omens and indicators say otherwise, think, wait, do not cross your arms, do not stand paralyzed, immobile, as if you had a thousand sacks of sand on your feet; insist, persevere, be grateful. The universe moves in our favor when we are grateful. Believing in your dreams means you can achieve that that you want, even if the arrows point in another direction.

Even if you think you do not have any talent, studies, abilities, money; when it's about money there is no need to worry, because there is much of it circulating in the universe. Yearn to have it, work to get it, but do it within the legal norms, those norms that do not harm anyone. Do not build an empire that's based on things that are detrimental to others, that our freedom does not affect that of others. If you want a career, whatever it is, study, if you want a car, an airplane, a company, an agency, whatever your dream, just believe it is yours, but remember that without effort, determination, persistence and continuous work, dreams do not come true. To find a treasure within a mine, you must first dig; if you search the bottom of the sea, the more valuable it is what you seek, the deeper you will need to swim or explore; if one wants to eat fish, or one fishes for it, or simpler, one can pay a high price to someone who already risked themselves and got their feet wet.

It is necessary to believe, and to at least invest the energy. Fight, everything is achieved with effort, temperance, seriousness, restraint; believe, keep hope, imagine that you must reach your home, but the waters of the river are preventing you from passing, wait, believe, the high currents will calm down, then you will be able to cross and reach your destination.

Dream, believe, but most importantly, put everything in from your end so that your dreams are reachable.

If you do not have a dream, it is very difficult to get it to be real, but it is not enough to dream. Sometimes we dream, but we do not give our dreams the attention they deserve. In my case, when I'm asleep and dreaming I pay attention, because they almost always become reality. Once I dreamed that my wallet was stolen, but I forgot it and I did not pay attention to it ... and guess what? About two months went by; someone snatched my wallet from me with everything in it, including the house keys. That happened in my home country.

When I speak of dreaming, I do not refer to those dreams, rather to the things we want to achieve in our life: to have an education and all the things that every human being would like to be able to obtain; those things that allow for greater comfort and quality of life. Everyone can dream and achieve; setting goals is people's right. You are not the exception to the rule; start working on what you would like to be or have, be sure to reinforce that power within you, perhaps you have not yet realized the potential within you. Believe in yourself, in your person; if you have to bet, then bet on what you can do. Nothing will be lost for trying; to think, to assist, though it is not enough, to believe in one self it means to know oneself as competent to develop oneself in any area, profession, business or roll that one chooses. Believe in yourself believe in your dreams.

Faith, Will, Enthusiasm, and Continuous Work, works wonders

Having faith in God is very important because it gives you strength, which maybe you would not have otherwise, if you totally lack it, faith in God, creator of the universe, has a power over you and everything you would like to have or accomplish, you must believe in yourself, have confidence in yourself, it serves as a push to achieve dreams, everyone has a potential that together with self-confidence, faith, and hope, it will help you walk the right path to get to where you want.

Never lose faith, be ardent of will, and enthusiasm, and use it as a rudder to push yourself to the top. Many people travel long distances to fulfill their dreams, and others have had to climb high mountains, but they have not given up, they have not given in to the hardships of the weather, that willpower that they possess within themselves, and that drives them. This disposition that emanates from their inner self makes them an increasingly strong entity; they are people who do not lose interest in reaching their dreams. They love themselves and their loved ones, love for themselves and their families, is also a driving force, leaving them no room to give up or look back. They continue to fight even when the waters are against them and the winds hit without mercy, that interest to conquer all that is beautiful and lovely in the universe, that voice that everyone carries inside and shouts to them from the inside, urging them to go forward, through every moment of their lives. Faith, will and enthusiasm are key pieces to challenge the onslaught and unexpected storms.

87

People who are worthy of admiration, and praise, whose will power is above any challenge and prognosis, embark on a journey towards great goals in search of unimaginable dreams. Who have decided to make way in the deep sea, have you thought what it means to try to make a path in the middle of the ocean? Let me tell you that people with a strong will and a mind full of positivism have known how to thresh the path on the waters, deserts and even in the clouds in search of an ideal, have set goals for themselves, and great ideals. But as I have said in previous topics, in any project, continuous work is necessary. You who are reading this book now, take the reins of your ship, begin to build a path that takes you to that fixed point you have drawn in your mind, transport yourself to where your dream is, do as those people do who with fervor and passion have fought and triumphed, having nothing in their hands, whose only tools have been their faith, will, enthusiasm, and continuous work.

Dear reader, I hope that this is neither your case or your story, but in case your strength is exhausted, if your enthusiasm, desire, courage are diminishing, it is time to get to your feet, to get up, to make your journey through life, the one that you and no one else can travel. Take strength from where there is none, even if it is from the soles of your feet, they do have an irresistible force, ask your feet how they can manage all the weight of your body, I already asked my own and I have followed their example, they never complain about the weight of the body, even if they are tired and exhausted and worn out, they keep walking until they reach their final destination. If you feel weak because of everyday problems, look at your feet, watch them carefully, do not let yourself be overwhelmed, do not let sadness fill your heart, tell your mind that you are strong; continue as the people in the olden days did, they walked even when knowing that their destination was far away, once they would make their decision to go somewhere they did not stop until they would arrive. If you feel that you cannot go any longer, take strength from the soles of your feet if necessary, only those who struggle incessantly, without stopping, resisting all the weight that life has given them, they have the opportunity and the happiness to be able to say "it was difficult, but I have succeeded. I have been crowned; I have the luxury of an awaited dream."

Coming out of the nothing

In my teenage years, I went to an outdoor campaign, on an esplanade, in my country, in my hometown; the campaign ended at 11:30 p.m., more or less. Three adult people accompanied me to my house, but we had to walk along a dark street, deserted, without street lighting, which still has no light because the residents are a ways from that street, there are no houses on the banks only trees, huge old oaks and huge mahogany woods, large foliage, a thicket towards the back side and a diversity of plants. There was no other option to enter the residential area and the nearby neighborhoods; one was forced to pass through the deserted street. When we were having to crossing a place where its darkness went beyond its borders, and where the people used to say that there were ghosts there, chickens with chicks at midnight, and then disappeared out of nowhere, the locals also used to tell that you could see headless people, and a countless number of things that I heard about since I was a little girl, but it was very difficult to believe, I thought it was just the people making it up, only to frighten others.

For me that was just stories or the imagination of people at work who dedicated their time to saying such things. I never thought that was possible, until that night when we were just getting there, out of nowhere in the darkness on the right side of the trees a rather large white dog formed itself out of nowhere. It was not my imagination, I saw it with my own eyes, at that moment I did not say anything about the dog, everyone was talking about the things that came out from there, the dog appeared at the exact moment I had just said, I'm not afraid, it was at that moment when the large, tall, and white as snow dog, crossed the street, but just before reaching the other side it disappeared, it vanished into thin air. I did not make any comments, because the people who were accompanying me had to return to their homes through the same street. I kept silent so not make them feel fear, because I did not know if they had seen that white dog that formed from nothing and disappeared in the same way. My allusion to this is only as a small reference, because as I saw that dog that came out of nowhere, many people around the world have formed out of nothing, with the only difference that they achieved great feats and have invested time, money among other things. Many people have achieved great victories in their lives, they have come out of nowhere, but they have been able to fight against the winds and the tides, and they have been able to realize their great dreams even above the fear, the darkness, and the disadvantages, with which they have stumbled on. With their struggles and efforts, they have defeated adversity. They have not let their dreams fade into nothingness, as how it happened with the white dog that I saw, and that it was not a dream, that was real, something I saw with my own eyes. Keeping ahead is for the brave, all the people who fight to the end with fervent desire, and enthusiasm overcoming fear. They are capable of getting ahead, even when lacking the help, many heroines and heroes who have managed to come out from the nothing, do not think that you cannot do it because of the lack of being able to study, or because you lack capacity, time or money, or lack of someone who will stretch out a helping hand, all over the world there are many people who are willing to support unconditionally, in any case if you do not find someone try yourself, come out of the dark, look up, a bright light awaits you to light your way and guide you on the right path, towards the realization of your dreams.

Everyone without exception has the same right to dream, and work to make it come true. Conquering goals is a right of every person, whenever things are done right, wherever you are, anywhere in the geography of the planet, get up, stand up, fight, get ready to get ahead, go in search of that future which awaits you, it can be in sports, education, fashion, business, literature, film, start throw in your little grain of sand, just as the sun shines and does not deny anyone it's splendor, all alike can dream and make those dreams come true, still coming out of the nowhere.

You have wings, even if you do not believe it

There are in the world a group of birds that fly as high as any human being could imagine, among them are the Indian goose, they are the ones that fly the highest, but she is not the only one; there is the vulture, the condor, the eagle and a series of birds that rise to greater heights, and then there is the swift, who maintains itself suspended in the air for almost three years without coming down to the ground nor to perch in any tree, this last one sleeps in the heights, they feed on flies and insects that fly in the air. These birds do not fear heights, they do not suffer from stress or frustration and if for any reason or cause they would fall, they do not remain stuck lamenting the fall.

They rapidly try to rise as quickly as possible. They have their strategies and mechanisms to go up and down, their skill and intelligence helps them overcome any obstacle and even obviate the predators, they have an incredible vision and agility, which allows them to stay in the heights. The wings that a human being has, without a fear of being mistaken, are more agile and much more powerful than those of these birds that live in the heights.

If you ask yourself, where are those wings of which I speak of? Or you would say that what I am saying is something absurd, no, you who is dedicating a little of your time reading my writings, here expressed, and all the people from any corner of the world, have the ability to fly as high as they propose, apart from any physical condition.

As I said in previous articles, it's enough with just creating an idea in one's mind, of course, be sure that your idea does not harm anyone and that it favors not only yourself, but that it contributes to a common good. That it goes to the benefit of the others, because if we incur something with the purpose of obtaining self benefits, but it is detrimental to others, at the end of the day we will have to pay a price, more if what we do goes in search of favor and improves lives, perhaps one will only have to pay the price of fame, but in the end one will have done something good in favor of humanity.

We all have the right and opportunity to fly as high as we want, it is unique to each person individually, although sometimes in a certain way, when it comes to achieving goals and dreams, it becomes a little more personal, you can take an animal to a beautiful and crystalline spring to drink water, but if this one is not thirsty, you will not be able to force it to drink from it. Even the triumphs of our children, can be persuaded, and influenced, but they have last word. We can create the basis for others to reach their dreams and guide them on a good path, but it is something very personal, you will not be able to lend your wings for someone to fly. If you want to achieve a dream do not waste time doubting whether it will turn out or not, if you set your mind to it, it's enough with having a dream in mind, a positive thoughts, a set of small wings that will be strengthened with effort, dedication, and work, put yourself on the waiting list. Because wings do not grow overnight, hardly anything is achieved. From one day to another few things can be achieved, everything needs some time. If we observe the offspring of the birds mentioned above, all without exception take time before they can fly, feathers start to develop and little by little their wings grow, until they are strong enough and able to fly they do not undertake their flight, some fall but they do not stop to whine and complain of the pain from the fall, they try to rise again quickly and take flight. People, all in general, with a few exceptions, possess a superior intelligence, ability of thought, reasoning, that power of thought that allows to discern between the good, the better and the less good. That if one takes advantage of them, they do not let themselves be overwhelmed by falls, and truncated flights, and they do not let themselves fall into despair of wanting to fly high and stay up without the fear of falling.

Put your wings to work, you have to, even though you have not thought of that, a mind that is unique to all human beings. Let yourself be guided by your imagination. Create a dream, whatever you want, everything is possible, not only birds can fly high, all who have triumphed and obtained great wealth, goods, titles, crowns, and high honors began with a dream, an idea to which they gave life to, history speaks of them, their personal story identifies them. They are great winners and conquerors; their wings propelled them as high as they had dreamed. You have wings, even if you do not believe it.

Keep your feet on the ground, even if you are a star

Keeping your feet firmly on the ground after you have been able to reach the highest peaks, to the pinnacle of success, could prove a little difficult for some people, but we have known of numbers of people throughout history and time, who have had the opportunity to be a star and to be as high as only stars can be, and to know of themselves there in the firmament as far as fame, success, money, material goods and wisdom are concerned, these are things that any mortal could feel so high on that perhaps they forget the human side of themselves, the fact is that most of those who have been and today still are at the peak of success, not only have been able to keep their feet on the ground even being so high, but have not dis-attached themselves from that human part despite the money, and the achievements. Many of these successful people have dedicated themselves to donating for charitable causes, in favor of children, hospitals, institutions for adults, many dedicate money and sometimes their time to sympathize with causes of countries, nations and other times they do so more individually with other people and organizations that perform non-profit social work. They have kept their feet well placed on the ground, despite belonging to the higher peaks and the larger societies. They have done so without any effort, because they understand that they are human like all others, and that despite the social condition of other people, in short, every human being belongs to the same category, that does not make us different, that of being a person.

You, just like others have already reached their dreams, have already climbed the mountain, are now up high next to the stars; keep your feet firmly on the ground, even if one is one of those stars with its own light and that for whatever reason do not need the heat from the sun, the presence of the moon, and much less the clarity of the day to shine, you have already reached the splendor and brilliance that only stars can have.

You have excelled, extraordinarily in your profession, business or in whatever your dream may have been, keep your feet on the ground, even if you are a star. Congratulations on not giving up on your dream.

You have an untold wealth

All human beings on the planet possess an incalculable wealth, which has nothing to do with purchasing power, with amounts of money. Money and all that can be bought contain a power; because without it you cannot get the things you need to live, and not only to live, but to be able to have quality of life.

It is true that in the world many children and adults lack the most essential things to live, that should not minimize their value as a person and or as a human being. All people have the same organs in the inside and on the outside, regardless of color or race, and that inner strength that you might not think is strong, but it is. Stand in front of a mirror, look at yourself for a few seconds, and you will see that as a person, you are just like all those who tread the earth without any exception. In case you have a condition, it does not place you below anyone, you are just as valuable as other people in the world. Think of yourself as a valuable being, possessing untold wealth. Nothing compares to you, so when it comes to moving forward to getting things, just like everyone else, you can get what your heart desires, regardless of whether you are a child, an adolescent, young, adult or a little older; you just need to have the desire, the strength and the decision. You have life, and with it you are already rich, because with that great and beautiful treasure, the rest will be secondary, as you already have your untold wealth, value it, many people do not believe that having life is something so valuable, nothing is worth more than life. If you are alive you have already triumphed, you are a winner, you have beat the other spermatozoids that fought with you before joining your mother's egg, that sure was a difficult thing, or have you never thought of that? You fought your first battle and were victorious, now that you are a person, it is easier to know that you are worth something because you are a person, and as such possesses an untold wealth.

Changing lives

Trying to change someone's life is a difficult task, because before thinking about changing someone, it is necessary for us, as people, to make a change in the way we act and or in some of the things that appear to be correct, but in short they are not, or to persuade another person to try and change their behavior or attitude, it is an arduous work, although it may be possible, all human beings are subject to change in one way or another.

This topic does not refer to urging people to change their way of being, although my work with different people over several years, has allowed me to influence some children, adolescents and adults to modify certain behaviors. Changing lives is rather a transformation in the lives of those who only need a tiny grain of sand to move forward. In this case it is a matter of urging someone, urging them to fight, to advance, to making efforts to succeed.

Put a quota on yourself, to go out looking for those who need it, maybe they do not need money, clothes or food, but a helping hand to take them for a few seconds, or to give a smile. A word of encouragement, guidance, an advice, an ear that can listen, a gesture of friendship and solidarity in those difficult moments, that in one way or another people, regardless of their social status or economic position, have to face, one can change the lives of others in many ways, throughout the world there are millions of people whose only dream is to fight and work to change the lives of those who suffer, angels in human clothing that travel the world with the intention to change the lives of thousands of children, adolescents, adults and old people, true heroes who remain anonymous, because their dream is to make others happy, because that is when they are also infinitely happy, full of joy and satisfaction, if we change even a single life, this will become a great cooperation and if we all unite as long as we can become a transforming entity, helping, contributing, with a grain of corn , it will grow and we will be able to reap big profits, not at an economical level, but at a human level, one of my dreams is that you, me, and everyone go after someone and change their life, because only then will we have a better society and a better world where we can all live in peace and tranquility. Changing lives through solidarity, cooperation, tolerance to the things that merit being tolerated, and love for our children and especially the elderly.

Changing lives, and encouraging others to move forward, and not give up on their dreams.

Change your reality with the power of your mind

The mind is a unique and infinite intellectual power, where all the thoughts, intentions, will, and all the psychic, conscious and unconscious cognitive processes live in it, although it is not an organ like the brain, the mind is able to travel to the most remote and unimaginable places that could exist and even to construct images and transport itself to those places that have never existed, in the mind the positive and negative thoughts are born, through which the human being can change their reality, their life, their environment, their city and that of other human beings. Your strength is able to modify a person's entire life, it will all depend on how you use it, if you think negatively, despair, discouragement, will destroy your life, but when you use it positively it will change all of your reality.

Someone of a playful spirit, willing to go forward, with purpose, insight, discernment and positive skills, is an excellent candidate to overcome all the battles that life presents them, and of course changes any reality as uncomfortable or difficult as it may be. You may be immersed in a world of loneliness, sadness, despair, stress, anxiety, resentment, emotional or physical pain due to illness, or other situations in which you think you will not be able to get out of, use your path opener, it is the only tool that you do not have to go to the store to buy and that you have it there at your disposal, at your reach, to be able to open holes where there are not even the slightest possibilities. This powerful tool is your mind, if you put your mind to work positively, all of your reality, all your surroundings as difficult and complicated as they are, will make such a positive change that, you yourself will hesitate a little to believe, change the way you think. Loneliness, sadness, illness and all those other things that serve as obstacles in the way, are just that, obstacles. And that all human beings can and do have the ability to remove them as debris from their lives.

Let a spark of energy, courage and joy flood your mind, do not rent more places in your life, your soul, your mind to sadness, discouragement, negativism, change your tenants, rent with purchase right to positivism, to value, happiness, love towards yourself, towards others, stop suffering because everything has a solution, open grooves with the power of your mind.

A positive and enthusiastic mind is able to heal the most serious of illnesses, to erase grudges from the soul, to heal wounds as deep as they might be, when one holds a grudge against someone for something that they have done to you, you are sitting them in a chair of honor, it is true that many people have had to go through unpleasant moments, for the daring and lack of consideration of other people, for situations that others have provoked. If you have been wronged do not give them so much privilege, when you hate someone or hold a grudge you are giving them a privileged place within your soul, your mind, your thoughts, take a step forward, abandon grudges, pain, sadness and disenchantment, think that only you have the power to change your whole life, your reality, turn your mind into a bright light, that enlightens everything around you and beyond, even if the clouds are present. Use your most powerful tool, the mind. It is the main axis that intervenes so that what we want can become reality. Do not allow negative thoughts to put you in a situation of doubt and disadvantage.

Even when you live in the world of the impossible, a thought full of positivism will make a change so great that you will be surprised at what you can achieve when the positive energies become in your favor, of course for everything a person wants one must invest some fees, investigate what you need to get to the goal, and go to work, get started. Do not allow negative thoughts to make nests in your mind, say no, but a resounding NO, cast into the void the negative and pessimistic thoughts, those thoughts of defeat that lead to no path.

When one gives rise to those thoughts, the path can be completely open and all the lights on, the only thing is that your mind is blocked and a mind in such a state is like one of those machineries that serve to clear the way and open a path where there is none, but that it is stuck in a swamp, and cannot get out of there neither, it cannot go forward or backwards. Defeatist thoughts, discouragement, and frustration should be stopped, they should be given a NO so large that they cannot sneak past even in the smallest of sense.

Make them understand that in your mind you do not have room for them to enter; only you decide if you open the door.

Imagine that you let into your house; all those who want to enter without your permission, in the same way that you would be letting in the thoughts of frustration and defeat, they only enter when someone allows them to enter. Stop mourning; change the reality of your existence. Your mind is an infinite, unlimited power that can break the most solid and exalted barriers that arise in your environment or in your life.

Believe that you can achieve success, abundance unlike any in everything you undertake, what you want to be and what you want to have. Change your reality with the power of your mind.

Dressed for success

In previous topics we have talked about the garments worn by warriors in the olden days.

Today, agents wear vests that protect them from dangers, firefighters wear their uniform that distinguishes them, many employees in different countries wear a uniform and also some students, the clothing must match the work being done, the place, the weather or the climate.

In some countries and regions the cold is intense in the winter and clothing must be adequate to the winter season, while in others that have tropical climate the temperature becomes variable. In short we must dress according to the function that we are going to perform or with which person we will be meeting.

And especially where we will be going, the clothes we use to go swimming at the beach with will never be the same that is used to sleep with, in some countries when a young woman is getting married she wears a white dress, each outfit must go according to the occasion, many people especially in countries of Hispanic origin, when they go to a funeral they usually wear black and white clothes. When going to an interview to apply for a job the clothing should go according to the work that will be performed. The athletes use different uniforms according to the sport they practice, the pilots and all the crew dress differently to the passengers, and what about the astronauts, they do indeed need a wardrobe that allows them to be able to rise and stay in space for the time they are required to stay on the ship. In everyday life chefs, they never wear the type of clothes that the diners wear, the racecar drivers; all are distinguished with their uniform. In general everyone dresses differently according to a number of factors and conditions that should be taken into account when choosing a wardrobe.

The reality is that for each occasion of our daily life we need clothes, on each occasion the garments will be different, so if we want to reach an achievement or a goal, the garment must go according to the goal being achieved. Dressing in the outfit worthy of the occasion is one of the main tools to achieve the dreams that we have and that we want them to come true. We must dress to triumph with an outfit that perhaps at first sight is hard to be seen, because it is different to what each person wears to cover up, or in some occasions to highlight their beauty, delicacy or simply because it is necessary to wear to keep your good health, or because the moment requires it.

The dress that we should all wear when it comes to triumph, the suit that I intend you to wear is that of a dream, it has nothing to do with the type of clothing that can be seen with the naked eye, and although different according to the customs of every nation or country, we should all wear the costumes of our dreams. I mean garments that are invaluable. That we cannot buy in any store and much less on the internet, nor outfits that cost a lot. It should be nothing we have to invest on, although sometimes it costs enough work and difficulty to keep them. Sometimes things in our lives get so complicated, that we find it hard to believe that we have such valuable clothes and that if we use them anywhere in the world we will go unnoticed.

WISDOM, almost all people have within them that brilliance, that if we go to the divine source, we will realize that we have it, and if you have wisdom, you have already taken the first step to developing an idea to be able to reach any dream that you have in your mind.

INTELLIGENCE, ability to understand and comprehend, most people around the world have intelligence, you do too, it has nothing to do with going to school, it is a gift that God has given for free, it can be developed at school level, it is there inside people, even when you have not been able to study, it is a unique virtue, that capacity to reason and think that it is only natural of human beings, that beautiful suit of yours, you may not have realized that you are intelligent, but you are, and with this garment there is nothing in the world that cannot be created, for the good and for the benefit of humanity, if your intelligence is asleep, awaken it, take it out in the fresh air, sometimes we put it away as we do with some piece of clothing, we keep it closed up, and without let it see the light of day.

Take it out, let it float, you will realize that you are as smart as those who have already realized their dreams, think of yours, surely there is one that belongs to you. Dress for success.

THOUGHT, all human beings have been given the privilege of being able to think, if you think and let your thinking arise by giving rein to your imagination, forming in your mind a great dream, a persistent and tenacious thought, combined with wisdom and intelligence, those outfits will not go out of style.

POSITIVE ATTITUDE, a good positive attitude, this garment that we should take with us to all places, be positive in the face of life, will give you that strength that is needed to move forward in case the obstacles and difficulties are present in the process while going in search of the realization of your dream. You who has long since sown in your head, but has not yet decided to develop it and give it life and a name, decide already, it is time to move forward without giving up.

CONSTANCE, this beautiful garment, is of great importance when dressing, being constant and firm not only embellishes us, and it encourages us in resolutions and in purposes.

PATIENCE, is a gift that not everyone can cultivate, because to most impatience characterizes them, even more so when they want to achieve a dream, almost all in this case want things like teenagers, in the here and now, but if we all propose it to ourselves all the people can dress in patience, it's free, it does not appear in any store, to achieve a goal a certain dose of patience is required, even to sow a small plant, everything needs a margin of time, patience is bitter, but its fruits are sweet . Bamboo is a plant that we have much to learn from, as far as patience is concerned, this tree gives us a good teaching, it takes its time, spreading its roots down into the earth. It is a plant different from other trees, instead of rising to the surface of the ground, like other plants do, after five years of silence hiding its roots, it has a kind of mystery, if the farmer is novel and does not know the growth process of this plant he could despair and desist from it, thinking that it has dried and that it will never grow tall. But an experienced sower knows that he must have patience and expect it to take its time. In the same way as bamboo, dreamers must learn that there are some dreams that are wanted to be reached, where time and patience are essential.

EFFORT must be part of the garments of a dreamer, everything requires a share of investment, and effort is included when you want to achieve something, you cannot leave the goals to time or chance, without any effort. Put on a necklace of faith, a hat of hope, a good suit made of an arduous and effective work, put on shoes of courage, effort, constancy, if you wear a ring make sure that it is one of responsibility, never forget a good perfume of patience. Because for all that is wanted in life one should have a margin of expectation. With all these beautiful accessories you are already dressed for success.

The impossible does not exist for those who dream

The word impossible is not in the dictionary of those who dream of reaching for the stars. It is true that they are as high as the firmament. Who says that the person with desire to advance, with courage, rage, risky motivation, with a vision of a winner cannot reach the unattainable? Nothing is impossible if you can believe. How far are the clouds? How high are the stars? They will never be so high that you cannot reach them or touch them with your hands. Not only can you embrace them as your own stars, if you propose it to yourself, you could also become one of them. For everything you want to do or have, you will have to apply a series of details and formats, to be taken into account when thinking about a goal.

To believe, to be motivated, to live with joy and enthusiasm, is not enough, a tenacious mind is one of the main tools, the foundation, is the driving force, but if you leave everything in your mind as is, without taking the action necessary to rise to where you want to go, no matter how positive your mind is, if you do not follow the right path by doing everything that is required to climb to the sky. Putting the thought in your mind is not enough; it is the first step it is just that looking at it from below without any action leads nowhere. Astronauts before going up to the moon, they have prepared first, if you want to be a star or simply have them in your power, you must know that some guidelines are required to be followed, whether it be getting to the moon, a mountain, reaching the sky, the clouds, the stars, or reaching the highest peak in the universe, or to overcome the challenges of life itself, if dreams and triumphs are left in thought, it could happen to them as like those trees that the wind blows away, they remain abandoned and left on the ground, without anyone to cut them or pick them up. Positive thinking is a very important link, but it needs work and effort, because ideas should not remain stagnant in the brain, they must be released, must be injected with life, given a body and a name.

Be a star or reach one of them. The impossible does not exist for the dreamer.

Modesta Mata

S he was born in the Dominican Republic, lives in the United States. She began as a preschool teacher at age 16; from that time she continued teaching from the first levels, intermediate and secondary. She worked at Corazón de Jesús College in Santo Domingo, where she also served as an administrative director. She worked for more than 15 years at the secondary school Juan Pablo Duarte as a psychologist for the young between 13 and 22 years old, she has worked for more than two decades offering counseling talks for adolescents. She worked in the armed forces of her country as an instructor (teacher) for more than seven years. In 2005, she founded the "INEVOMA" Vocational Guidance and Evaluation Institute, aimed at offering counseling and vocational guidance to high school students, in order to guide them in choosing a university career. In the same, they offered: behavior modification, techniques of study habits and education in values.

Thinker, composer of music, is a member of the General Society of Dominican authors, composers and publishers of music, INC.

She has written more than 200 poems and songs, "the illusion of seeing you", "you have your life", "it was not you", "tell me now", "I do not feel anything for you anymore", "I live and die" "You put dynamite to my senses", "adhered to you", "an evening", "if I wanted to", "I will have to pay the price", "your love is like quicksand", "heart and reason" among others.

She is a psychologist and a member of the Dominican school of psychologists of the Dominican Republic CO-

DOPSI. She wrote several online self-help articles for Re-alidades Magazine in New York. She has also written for the newspaper The Change in West New York, such as "be different," "positive and liberating love," "friendship," "let's recover our values."

She is the author of the book "Beautiful Sunrise", which reflects the diversity of life. Poems and phrases to reflect, offers a message of encouragement, strength and motivation.

Made in the USA
Middletown, DE
21 July 2017